The Future of Finance:
How AI Will Revolutionize Your Job and Make You Obsolete

Written By:
Hudson Budrick III

Copyright 2024
All Rights Reserved

Table of Contents

1. **Introduction: The Rise of AI in Finance**

    - Understanding the AI revolution in finance
    - Why AI is not just a passing trend, but a transformative force

2. **AI in Finance: What It Means for Your Job**

    - How AI is reshaping financial roles
    - Key areas of finance being impacted by AI

3. **AI and Data: The New Currency in Finance**

    - The importance of data in AI-driven financial decision-making
    - How AI processes and interprets vast datasets

4. **AI in Portfolio Management: Automating Asset Allocation**
    - The rise of algorithmic trading and robo-advisors
    - How AI enhances portfolio optimization and diversification

5. **AI in Risk Management: Predicting and Mitigating Financial Risks**
    - AI's ability to predict market volatility and financial risks
    - How AI helps firms improve risk-adjusted returns

6. **AI-Driven Analytics: Revolutionizing Financial Decision-Making**
    - AI's role in predictive analytics, sentiment analysis, and decision support
    - Leveraging AI to uncover hidden insights from financial data

7. **AI and Behavioral Biases: The End of Human Error?**
    - How AI helps reduce biases in financial decision-making
    - Real-world examples of AI overcoming human errors

8. **Job Displacement and Transformation: Will AI Replace You?**

- Understanding the threat of job displacement
- How AI is creating new roles and reshaping traditional finance jobs

9. The Hybrid Workforce: Collaborating with AI

- How human and machine collaboration is the future of finance
- The importance of developing a symbiotic relationship with AI

10. AI Tools and Techniques for Finance Professionals

- A guide to the most popular AI tools and technologies in finance
- How to incorporate AI into your daily workflow

11. AI and Risk-Adjusted Returns: Outperforming Human Analysts

- How AI outperforms human analysts in risk-adjusted returns
- Case studies and data showing AI's superior performance

12. How to Prevent Becoming Obsolete in Your Finance Job: Embrace AI and Become a Top-Tier Employee or Risk Manager

- Steps to remain relevant in an AI-powered world
- Developing AI literacy and collaboration skills
- Leveraging AI tools to enhance your performance

13. Conclusion: Thriving in the AI-Powered Future of Finance

- o Summarizing the key points
- o Embracing AI as a tool for career growth and success in finance
- o The future of finance as a collaboration between humans and AI

Chapter 1: Introduction: The Future is Now

Welcome to the Age of AI

The year is 2024, and if you're reading this, you've probably already heard about Artificial Intelligence (AI) revolutionizing industries from healthcare to entertainment, logistics to education. But when it comes to finance—the world of spreadsheets, financial statements, stock market analysis, and investment portfolios—AI's influence has been nothing short of transformative. AI isn't just on the horizon anymore—it's here, reshaping your daily tasks, your job roles, and, ultimately, the very nature of finance itself.

AI-powered tools like robo-advisors, algorithmic trading, and predictive analytics have already begun to infiltrate financial services, changing the way institutions operate and the roles that finance professionals occupy. For those who have spent years mastering traditional financial methods, this wave of change can feel daunting. You might even be wondering: *How much longer will my skills remain relevant?*

In this chapter, we'll begin by exploring the rapid evolution of AI, how it's changing finance today, and why it's set to make entire job functions obsolete. It's not a matter of "if" AI will impact your career—it's a question of when and how you will need to adapt to this new reality.

The Changing Landscape of Work

You might recall a time when "robots" in finance meant nothing more than automated systems for executing trades at high speeds or perhaps a calculator replacing your paper-and-pencil ledger. But the reality now is much more complex—and much more pervasive.

In the early days of AI, systems required vast human intervention. An algorithm had to be carefully crafted, tested, and then manually adjusted by an expert. Today, however, we have machines that are not only *self-learning*, but also capable of making real-time decisions based on vast quantities of data—faster and more accurately than any human could ever manage.

The emergence of AI is not just about replacing simple tasks—it's about redefining entire workflows and industries. And finance, as an industry built on data analysis, risk assessment, forecasting, and decision-making, is uniquely vulnerable to this technological disruption.

In this chapter, we'll examine how the financial services industry is adapting to the digital transformation, and how traditional roles are being challenged. You may already have a sense of this shift, but what you might not realize is just how fast it's happening—and how deep this transformation goes. It's not just about replacing your job; it's about creating a completely new landscape where the rules are changing and the tools are evolving.

The Rise of AI in Finance

To understand why AI is such a game-changer for finance professionals, we first need to understand its rise in the industry. Artificial intelligence isn't just a new trend; it's a massive shift that has been building for years.

Let's break it down:

- **Machine Learning and Predictive Analytics**: In finance, machine learning (ML) algorithms are used to analyze historical data and make predictions about future market trends. These predictive models can help identify risk factors, forecast investment returns, or even create more personalized financial strategies for individual clients. The key advantage is that these models don't just "calculate" based on preset conditions—they learn from data, adapting as markets change.

- **Automated Trading**: Once confined to quantitative analysts or "quants," AI has now taken over the world of algorithmic and high-frequency trading. In fact, more than 60% of all stock market trades are now executed by algorithms. AI-driven trading systems analyze massive amounts of market data at lightning speed, buying and selling stocks, bonds, and commodities with precision. While human traders are still involved in strategy and oversight, AI increasingly handles the execution of trades in real-time, making decisions faster and more accurately than any human could.

- **Robo-Advisors and Portfolio Management**: Perhaps the most visible manifestation of AI in retail finance is the rise of robo-advisors—automated platforms that provide financial advice based on algorithms and customer data. These systems have disrupted traditional wealth management by offering low-cost, automated portfolio management for retail investors. Unlike human advisors, robo-advisors don't suffer from bias, fatigue, or inconsistent performance. They offer scalable, data-driven solutions that can quickly adapt to changing market conditions, serving millions of clients simultaneously.

- **Fraud Detection and Security**: AI-powered systems can spot patterns in financial transactions to identify unusual behavior or fraud in real time. Traditional fraud detection models relied on predefined rules and risk factors, but AI takes a more dynamic approach. Machine learning can continuously adapt and improve, detecting new types of fraud that humans might miss.

- **Customer Service Automation**: Through the rise of AI-driven chatbots, customer service in the finance world is becoming faster, more responsive, and more efficient. These virtual assistants can handle everything from answering basic questions to processing transactions, leaving human agents free to focus on more complex tasks. While this shift is still in its early stages, the future of AI-powered customer interaction is already here, and it's expected to eliminate the need for large teams of human customer service agents in the near future.

A Brief History of AI in Finance

Artificial intelligence has been around for decades, but its integration into finance is a relatively recent phenomenon. Let's take a quick look at how we got here:

- **1950s-1970s**: Early AI research focuses on rule-based systems and basic computer programs that can assist in tasks like calculations. In finance, the first computers were used to manage transactions and perform simple calculations. However, these systems were far too primitive to have a profound impact on the industry.

- **1980s-1990s**: The rise of personal computers and the development of software tools like spreadsheets revolutionized finance. However, AI remained a niche technology in the hands of a few specialized analysts. Trading algorithms were developed, but they were still rudimentary and heavily reliant on human oversight.

- **2000s-Present**: The explosion of big data, powerful computational systems, and advances in machine learning algorithms has made AI indispensable in finance. Today, AI is used for everything from high-frequency trading to credit scoring, risk management, fraud detection, and customer relationship management. As data storage and processing capabilities continue to expand, AI's influence is only going to grow.

- **2020s and Beyond**: The future of AI in finance is poised to redefine how the industry operates. As machine learning models become more sophisticated, the industry is moving toward full automation in many aspects of trading, investment management, and even regulatory compliance. The next decade will likely see the near-total replacement of certain human jobs by AI—especially in roles related to data analysis, back-office operations, and transaction processing.

Why You Need to Pay Attention

By now, you may be wondering: *How is this going to affect my job in finance?*

The reality is, if you're a finance professional, AI will likely impact your career in one of two ways:

1. **Replacement of Routine Tasks**: Many of the tasks you perform daily—such as analyzing financial reports, forecasting trends, or performing risk assessments—can now be handled by AI algorithms. AI doesn't get tired, doesn't make errors due to oversight, and can process data at speeds no human can match. These are tasks that once took hours or even days but are now reduced to seconds.

2. **Complete Displacement of Certain Roles**: As AI continues to grow in sophistication, entire job functions will be eliminated. For example, traditional roles like financial analysts, tax accountants, and even investment advisors are increasingly at risk. The algorithms and systems that power AI can take over much of the decision-making process in these roles, leaving little room for human intervention.

But this isn't all doom and gloom. While certain jobs will disappear, new opportunities will emerge. There will be a greater need for professionals who can design, manage, and supervise AI systems. The roles of data scientists, AI specialists, and machine learning engineers are expected to grow rapidly in finance.

Facing the Future with Optimism

As you move through this book, you'll come to understand that AI is not an enemy but an inevitable part of your future. Rather than being something to fear, it's something to embrace. AI will help streamline your work, free you from mundane tasks, and enable you to focus on more high-level, strategic aspects of finance. But only if you're ready for it.

In the coming chapters, we'll dive deeper into the specific AI tools that will likely replace your role, and more importantly, how you can prepare for this future—whether that means acquiring new skills, shifting career paths, or understanding how to work alongside AI to your advantage.

Welcome to the AI-driven future of finance. It's going to be an exciting ride—but only if you're prepared to evolve with it.

Chapter 2: The Rise of AI in Finance

The Genesis of AI and Its Transformation in Finance

Artificial Intelligence has evolved from being a speculative concept to a transformative tool that is reshaping entire industries, and finance is no exception. While AI is often associated with futuristic technology, its roots go back several decades, and its influence in finance is more profound than many realize. In this chapter, we'll explore the rapid evolution of AI, particularly in the finance sector, and how it's revolutionizing the way finance professionals work.

AI's journey in finance is one of both gradual integration and sudden breakthroughs. Early attempts at automating financial tasks were rudimentary at best, limited to basic computational assistance. Today, AI not only automates routine tasks, but also drives complex decision-making processes, enhances forecasting accuracy, and powers entirely new business models.

Before diving into specific tools and applications, it's important to understand the foundational principles that have fueled AI's rise within the financial services industry.

A Brief History of Artificial Intelligence in Finance

To grasp the extent of AI's impact on finance, we need to start by looking at the history of AI development itself. While the broad concept of "artificial intelligence" has been around for centuries, its practical application in finance began much more recently.

1. **The Early Days: Rule-Based Systems (1950s-1970s)**

    - **The Birth of AI**: The term "Artificial Intelligence" was coined by John McCarthy in the 1950s, but the practical applications of AI were very limited in the early days. During this period, financial institutions primarily relied on simple computers for data processing and basic calculation tasks.

    - **Rule-Based Systems**: In finance, the earliest AI-like systems were essentially rule-based models, where specific "if-then" conditions were programmed into the system. These systems could process transactions and reconcile accounts but were relatively inflexible.

- o **Limitations**: While early computers could automate certain simple tasks, they lacked the ability to learn from data or adapt to changing conditions.

2. **The Rise of Expert Systems and Quantitative Models (1980s-1990s)**

    - o **Expert Systems**: The 1980s saw the development of "expert systems," which were designed to replicate the decision-making ability of human experts in specific fields. These systems were based on large sets of rules that mimicked the reasoning and judgment of experienced financial professionals.

    - o **Algorithmic Trading**: By the late 1980s and 1990s, the finance industry began experimenting with more sophisticated systems for quantitative trading and investment management. The introduction of financial derivatives and the growing complexity of financial markets pushed institutions to adopt algorithms for pricing and risk management.

    - o **Market Data Analysis**: In this era, finance professionals began using more advanced statistical models to analyze financial data. These models, often grounded in econometrics and statistics, could predict market trends and inform investment strategies. However, these were still "static" models that didn't adapt or learn.

3. **Machine Learning and Big Data (2000s-Present)**

    - o **The Machine Learning Revolution**: With the advent of machine learning in the 2000s, the true transformative potential of AI in finance began to emerge. Unlike rule-based systems, machine learning models could learn from vast amounts of data, recognize patterns, and improve their predictions over time without requiring explicit reprogramming.

- **Big Data**: As the amount of data generated by financial markets, consumer transactions, and global economic indicators exploded, machine learning algorithms became the key to unlocking insights from this vast sea of information. The ability to process big data and extract actionable insights is one of the main reasons AI has gained such a dominant position in finance.

- **AI's Real-World Impact**: Today, AI powers everything from robo-advisors to credit scoring, fraud detection to portfolio management. Rather than simply automating existing processes, AI is enabling financial institutions to rethink how they do business entirely. It's not just about efficiency anymore—it's about creating smarter, more adaptive systems that can outpace traditional human decision-making.

Key Drivers of AI in Finance

The rise of AI in finance isn't just a matter of technological innovation. Several key factors have fueled its rapid adoption and transformation of the industry:

1. **Data Explosion**:

    - The sheer volume of data generated by financial markets, consumer behaviors, and transactional records has reached unprecedented levels. AI and machine learning thrive in data-rich environments because they rely on vast datasets to identify trends, patterns, and insights that were previously invisible to human analysts.

- **Example**: In trading, AI can process and analyze vast quantities of market data in real-time—stock prices, news feeds, social media sentiment, economic reports—allowing for much faster and more accurate decision-making than human traders.

2. **Increased Computational Power**:
    - The rapid advancement of computing hardware has made it possible to process complex AI models in real-time. In particular, Graphics Processing Units (GPUs) and specialized hardware like Tensor Processing Units (TPUs) have allowed AI models to learn and operate much faster than in the past.

    - **Example**: High-frequency trading systems powered by AI can execute thousands of trades in milliseconds, capitalizing on tiny fluctuations in the market that are undetectable to human traders.

3. **Algorithmic and Predictive Models**:

    - AI-driven predictive models have revolutionized how financial institutions forecast risk, assess creditworthiness, and even manage portfolios. These models are able to take into account a vast array of factors, including historical performance, market conditions, and even unconventional data sources like social media sentiment.

    - **Example**: Hedge funds use machine learning algorithms to analyze massive datasets from global markets, economic indicators, and even weather patterns to make real-time investment decisions.

4. **Cost Efficiency and Automation**:

    - One of the primary reasons AI has exploded in finance is its potential to reduce costs through automation. Tasks that once required hundreds or even thousands of human workers—such as transaction monitoring, compliance reporting, and fraud detection—can now be automated using AI systems, improving efficiency and reducing the risk of human error.

- **Example**: Robo-advisors have dramatically reduced the cost of financial advice by automating portfolio management and personalizing investment strategies for individual clients with little or no human involvement.

5. **Consumer Expectations and Demand**:

    - With the rise of AI-powered consumer products and services (like personalized recommendations on Netflix or Amazon), consumers now expect a high level of personalization and instant responsiveness. Financial services companies have been forced to adapt, leveraging AI to offer personalized financial planning, real-time updates on portfolio performance, and more immediate customer service.

    - **Example**: AI-powered chatbots, such as those used by banks, allow customers to interact with their financial institution 24/7 for inquiries about balances, transactions, or even financial advice.

AI's Current Applications in Finance

AI's influence in finance is already being felt across a wide range of areas. Let's take a look at the most prominent AI-driven innovations:

1. **Algorithmic Trading and High-Frequency Trading (HFT)**:

    o   AI's ability to process vast amounts of market data quickly has given rise to algorithmic trading, where machines can execute buy and sell orders in real-time based on pre-defined strategies. High-frequency trading (HFT) takes this one step further by executing large volumes of orders in fractions of a second, taking advantage of small price changes that humans can't detect in time.

    o   **Impact**: This has led to the decline of traditional stockbrokers and manual trading, as AI is able to execute trades at much faster speeds and with greater accuracy.

2. **Robo-Advisors**:

    o   Robo-advisors are AI-powered platforms that automate the process of financial advising. Using algorithms, they assess an individual's risk tolerance, financial goals, and other factors to generate a personalized investment portfolio. Some robo-advisors also offer financial planning advice, tax optimization strategies, and rebalancing based on market conditions.

    o   **Impact**: The widespread use of robo-advisors has democratized wealth management, making it more accessible and affordable for a larger number of people.

3. **Credit Scoring and Risk Management**:

    o   AI has transformed how financial institutions assess credit risk. Machine learning algorithms can analyze a far broader range of data than traditional credit scoring models—such as payment history, spending patterns, and even social media activity—to predict the likelihood of a borrower defaulting on a loan.

- **Impact**: This has enabled lenders to make more accurate credit assessments, offering loans to a wider pool of potential borrowers while reducing the risk of defaults.

4. **Fraud Detection**:

    - Machine learning systems have revolutionized fraud detection by analyzing millions of transactions in real-time, flagging potentially fraudulent activity based on patterns and anomalies. These systems continually learn from new data to improve their detection capabilities and adapt to evolving fraud tactics.
    - **Impact**: AI has significantly reduced financial fraud and the manual effort required to detect fraudulent transactions.

5. **Personalized Customer Experiences**:

    - AI's ability to analyze customer behavior has led to more personalized financial experiences. AI tools can recommend personalized financial products, optimize investment portfolios based on individual needs, and offer real-time financial advice based on a customer's financial history and preferences.
    - **Impact**: This has created a more tailored experience for clients, improving customer satisfaction and increasing customer loyalty.

Why AI Is Here to Stay in Finance

It's clear that AI is not just a passing trend—it's a fundamental shift that is here to stay. The reason for this is simple: AI provides capabilities that traditional financial methods simply cannot match in terms of speed, scalability, and adaptability. As the volume of financial data continues to grow, and as consumer expectations continue to rise, the financial services industry will only become more reliant on AI to stay competitive.

While some finance professionals may feel threatened by these advancements, it's crucial to understand that AI is not a replacement but a tool that can enhance your work. In the next chapter, we will explore the specific tools and systems that are replacing many traditional tasks in finance, and how you can adapt to stay ahead of the curve.

AI is transforming finance—and those who embrace it will be well-positioned to thrive in the future.

Chapter 3: The AI Tools That Will Replace You

In the previous chapter, we explored the rise of AI in finance and the key drivers behind its rapid adoption. Now, it's time to get into the heart of the matter: the specific AI tools that are revolutionizing the financial services industry—and how they are increasingly replacing the roles that finance professionals have long occupied.

The truth is, many of the tasks and responsibilities that have traditionally filled your workday are already being automated by AI. What does this mean for your job? Will it be replaced entirely, or will there still be a place for you in this new AI-powered world?

In this chapter, we'll break down the key AI-driven technologies that are reshaping finance, making many traditional roles obsolete, and offering a glimpse into what the future holds for finance professionals.

1. Algorithmic Trading: The Dawn of a New Age in Trading

What it is:
Algorithmic trading, often referred to as algo-trading, involves the use of computer algorithms to execute buy or sell orders at optimal times based on predetermined criteria. These criteria can range from technical indicators, market sentiment, and price patterns, to more complex calculations based on machine learning and artificial intelligence.

In traditional trading, human traders made decisions based on their analysis of market conditions and news. However, AI systems can now analyze vast amounts of data in real-time and execute trades at speeds and with precision far beyond human capabilities. High-frequency trading (HFT), a subset of algorithmic trading, takes this a step further by executing thousands—or even millions—of trades per second based on minute fluctuations in the market.

How it replaces you:
In the past, stockbrokers, traders, and even hedge fund analysts were tasked with monitoring markets, conducting technical analysis, and making trading decisions. Today, AI-driven algorithms can perform these tasks automatically, constantly learning from market data and improving their predictive capabilities.

AI-powered trading systems don't need to take breaks, don't make emotional decisions, and are able to process market information in real-time at a scale and speed that humans simply can't match. For finance professionals, this means the traditional roles of stock traders, portfolio managers, and even risk analysts are at risk of being replaced by AI systems. Many financial institutions now rely on AI to optimize trade execution, manage portfolios, and even predict market movements.

Impact:

- **Job loss risk**: Human traders, especially those involved in high-frequency or quantitative trading, are increasingly being replaced by AI.

- **Opportunity for collaboration**: While AI handles the data-heavy, real-time decision-making, traders and analysts will need to shift to higher-level tasks such as strategy development, oversight, and managing AI systems.

2. Robo-Advisors: Goodbye to Human Financial Advisors?

What it is:
Robo-advisors are AI-powered platforms that provide automated investment advice based on algorithms. Using data such as age, risk tolerance, financial goals, and market conditions, robo-advisors build and manage personalized investment portfolios for individuals—without any human interaction.

These platforms use sophisticated algorithms to allocate assets in a way that minimizes risk and maximizes potential returns, all while continuously adjusting portfolios as markets shift. The rise of robo-advisors has democratized wealth management by offering low-cost, automated investment solutions for individuals who might not have the resources to hire a traditional financial advisor.

How it replaces you:
Traditionally, financial advisors have spent their careers offering personalized advice based on an individual's financial situation, risk tolerance, and life goals. They would analyze investment opportunities, advise on tax strategies, and adjust portfolios in response to market changes.

AI-powered robo-advisors have rendered many of these tasks automated and more efficient. These systems can continuously monitor the financial landscape, adjust portfolios, and offer tailored advice without human involvement. This eliminates the need for a traditional financial advisor for the majority of retail clients.

Impact:

- **Job loss risk**: The demand for human financial advisors is shrinking, especially in retail and mass-market wealth management. Robo-advisors handle asset allocation, risk assessment, and even tax optimization.

- **Opportunity for collaboration**: Financial professionals who want to stay relevant will need to focus on providing value beyond what AI can offer. Roles may shift toward more complex financial planning for high-net-worth individuals or those requiring bespoke services.

3. AI-Powered Risk Management Systems

What it is:
Risk management has always been a core function of finance, involving the identification, assessment, and mitigation of risks in investment portfolios and financial strategies. AI-powered risk management systems take this a step further by using machine learning and big data to identify potential risks more quickly and accurately than traditional models.

These systems can analyze massive datasets, including market data, economic indicators, and even unconventional data like social media sentiment or geopolitical news, to forecast risks in real-time. AI models can detect patterns that may indicate rising risks—such as potential defaults or liquidity crises—and take action to mitigate these risks automatically.

How it replaces you:
Historically, risk managers and analysts would spend hours or days sifting through financial reports, economic data, and market news to assess risk levels and determine appropriate actions. AI-powered risk

management systems do this in seconds, with much more comprehensive data and predictive accuracy. These systems can handle everything from credit risk and liquidity risk to operational and cybersecurity risks, automatically adjusting strategies as new data comes in.

Impact:

- **Job loss risk**: Risk analysts, especially those focused on routine tasks like data gathering, compliance reporting, or assessing market conditions, are increasingly replaced by AI systems.

- **Opportunity for collaboration**: Risk professionals will need to shift their focus to more strategic roles, overseeing AI models, managing the ethical implications of algorithmic decision-making, and providing human judgment on complex risk situations that AI may struggle to assess.

4. Natural Language Processing (NLP): Automating Research, Reporting, and Compliance

What it is:
Natural Language Processing (NLP) is a branch of AI focused on enabling machines to understand, interpret, and generate human language. In finance, NLP is being used to automate tasks like financial reporting, legal document analysis, regulatory compliance checks, and market sentiment analysis.

NLP algorithms can analyze vast amounts of unstructured data from sources like news articles, earnings reports, press releases, social media feeds, and analyst calls. They can quickly extract relevant information, identify key trends, and even summarize or generate reports in natural language. For example, a financial analyst might use an AI-powered NLP tool to scan quarterly reports and extract key data points, summarizing the performance of a company in seconds.

How it replaces you:
The traditional role of a financial analyst or researcher often involves reviewing large volumes of unstructured data, including news reports, SEC filings, and earnings calls. This work is time-consuming and tedious. AI-powered NLP tools can now perform these tasks automatically, extracting key insights and even drafting initial reports or compliance documentation.

Additionally, NLP is used in regulatory compliance, helping firms quickly identify potential violations, analyze contract language, and ensure adherence to financial laws—all tasks that once required human oversight.

Impact:

- **Job loss risk**: Financial analysts and compliance officers, especially those focused on manual data gathering and routine analysis, are at high risk of displacement.

- **Opportunity for collaboration**: Professionals will need to shift to higher-value tasks such as synthesizing AI-generated reports, interpreting findings, and making strategic decisions that AI cannot yet handle.

5. Customer Service Automation: AI-Powered Chatbots and Virtual Assistants

What it is:
AI-driven chatbots and virtual assistants are transforming customer service in finance. These AI-powered tools can handle a variety of customer inquiries, from account balance checks and transaction details to loan applications and basic financial advice.

AI chatbots are becoming increasingly sophisticated, capable of understanding and responding to complex customer requests, often in multiple languages. Financial institutions like banks, insurance companies, and fintech firms are deploying these chatbots to provide instant, round-the-clock customer support, allowing human agents to focus on more complex tasks.

How it replaces you:
Historically, customer service representatives have played a critical role in assisting clients, answering queries, and processing requests. As AI chatbots become more intelligent, these roles are being automated, reducing the need for human agents in many customer-facing positions.

These AI systems can answer frequently asked questions, assist with account management, and even help customers understand their financial products—all without any human intervention. As a result, many customer service and support roles in finance are being replaced by AI-powered systems.

Impact:

- **Job loss risk**: Customer service roles, particularly those dealing with routine inquiries or transactional support, are being automated by AI.

- **Opportunity for collaboration**: While chatbots and virtual assistants handle basic queries, human agents will be required to manage more complex customer relationships, troubleshoot unique issues, and offer personalized solutions.

Conclusion: Adapting to the AI Revolution

As we've explored in this chapter, AI is rapidly automating many tasks in finance that were once the domain of skilled professionals. Algorithmic trading, robo-advisors, AI-powered risk management, NLP, and customer service automation are all displacing traditional roles and tasks. But the story doesn't end there.

While some jobs will become obsolete, new opportunities are emerging for those who are willing to adapt. AI will not replace the need for human expertise in finance entirely. Instead, it will shift the focus from routine, data-driven tasks to higher-level decision-making, strategy, and human judgment.

In the next chapter, we'll explore the opportunities AI creates and how you can re-skill and adapt to ensure your place in the future of finance. Whether it's managing AI systems, analyzing complex data, or providing strategic insights, the key will be learning how to work alongside AI, rather than trying to compete with it.

Chapter 4: Embracing the Future: How to Stay Relevant in an AI-Driven Finance World

As we've seen in the previous chapters, AI is not just an additional tool in the financial services sector; it's a force that is reshaping the very nature of how finance works. From automating high-frequency trading to providing real-time risk management, AI is swiftly taking over many of the tasks that once defined finance jobs. For many professionals, this shift can feel daunting or even threatening. If AI is becoming so advanced, will there still be a place for human workers in the finance industry? And if so, what will that role look like?

The reality is that AI will likely not make finance professionals obsolete, but rather shift the nature of their jobs. **The key to surviving—and thriving—in this new world is adaptation.** In this chapter, we'll explore how finance professionals can not only survive the AI revolution, but also seize the opportunities that come with it. We'll cover the skills you need to develop, the new roles you should prepare for, and how to build a mindset that embraces AI as a partner, rather than a threat.

1. Shift from Routine Tasks to Strategic Oversight

One of the most important shifts you'll need to make in an AI-powered finance landscape is moving away from routine tasks and toward strategic oversight and decision-making. AI excels at processing massive amounts of data and identifying patterns in real-time, but it still lacks the human qualities of creativity, intuition, and judgment that are critical for higher-level decision-making. Here's how you can refocus your career:

- **Become an AI Liaison**: The future of finance will involve collaboration between AI systems and human decision-makers. As an expert in finance, you're well-positioned to be the bridge between AI and strategy. This means understanding how AI systems operate, interpreting their outputs, and applying those insights to broader business objectives. The AI systems will generate data and insights, but it will be your job to synthesize this information into actionable strategies.

- **Engage in Complex Problem Solving**: AI can help solve certain problems efficiently, but it is still far from perfect. It's the nuanced, unpredictable problems where human judgment comes in. For example, while AI may be able to forecast market movements, it can't fully account for human behavior, geopolitical events, or sudden shifts in market sentiment. Your role will shift toward providing insights on these complex, multifaceted problems.

- **Focus on Strategy and Risk Management**: AI is fantastic at identifying potential risks and opportunities, but it needs guidance from experienced professionals to understand context, interpret results, and make strategic decisions. Whether you're in portfolio management or risk analysis, your role will be about overseeing AI tools, ensuring they align with business goals, and using them to make more informed, strategic decisions.

Example: In the world of wealth management, AI can automate much of the investment decision-making process, but a human advisor will still be needed to understand the client's unique goals and emotional preferences. The role of financial advisors will evolve into relationship managers who leverage AI insights to provide personalized, holistic advice.

2. Learn to Work Alongside AI: Upskilling and Reskilling

While AI may take over many tasks, it can also be a powerful tool to augment your capabilities. The key to staying relevant in an AI-driven finance world is upskilling—learning to work alongside AI rather than viewing it as a threat.

Here's how you can upskill to stay ahead:

- **Understand AI and Machine Learning**: The most valuable skill you can acquire is an understanding of how AI and machine learning algorithms work. This doesn't mean you need to become a data scientist or AI developer, but gaining a basic understanding of how these systems work and how to interpret their outputs will be crucial. Familiarize yourself with concepts like supervised vs. unsupervised learning, neural networks, natural language processing (NLP), and deep learning. There are numerous online courses, certifications, and resources for learning AI fundamentals.

- **Data Literacy and Analytics Skills**: AI thrives on data, so becoming comfortable with data analysis is vital. Whether you're interpreting financial models or assessing the outputs of a machine learning model, having a solid grasp of data analytics tools and techniques will allow you to better understand and leverage AI systems. Learn to use platforms like Python, R, or even specialized finance tools like Bloomberg Terminal, which are increasingly integrating AI-powered data analytics.

- **Develop Soft Skills**: As AI handles more of the routine, transactional, and data-heavy work, the value of soft skills will become even more pronounced. Communication, emotional intelligence, and creativity are all qualities that AI cannot replicate. Finance professionals will need to refine these abilities in order to provide the human touch that clients expect, especially when dealing with complex financial strategies or emotional financial decisions.

Example: Financial analysts who can interpret AI-generated data and present it in a clear, actionable way will have a competitive edge. A deep understanding of finance combined with the ability to communicate complex findings to non-technical stakeholders will make you indispensable.

3. Embrace AI in Your Daily Work

To make the most of AI, start using it in your daily tasks. Don't wait for AI to "replace" your job—find ways to use it as a tool that enhances your own performance. The more familiar you are with these tools, the more proficient you will become at leveraging them for your advantage.

- **Automate Mundane Tasks**: Many of the routine tasks that AI is replacing—such as data entry, basic analysis, and generating reports—can be automated using AI tools. Look for ways to incorporate these technologies into your daily workflow to free up more time for strategic, value-added activities.

- **AI-Powered Research**: Use AI-powered tools to quickly sift through vast amounts of data, news, or financial statements. Tools that use natural language processing (NLP) can help you analyze market sentiment or identify emerging trends by scanning news outlets, social media, and analyst reports. You can also use AI-driven platforms like Bloomberg Terminal or Thomson Reuters to streamline your financial research.

- **AI for Portfolio Management**: Many asset management and wealth management firms are already using AI tools to help with asset allocation and portfolio management. While you may not be able to replace the human touch entirely, you can use AI to improve the precision of portfolio recommendations, forecast market conditions, and tailor financial advice based on AI-driven insights.

Example: Robo-advisors and AI algorithms are already transforming the investment landscape, but that doesn't mean wealth managers are obsolete. By understanding how these algorithms work, a human advisor can provide clients with more nuanced recommendations based on both AI-generated insights and the advisor's professional judgment.

4. Explore Emerging Roles in AI and Finance

While certain roles are becoming automated, new opportunities are emerging in the AI-driven finance world. As the financial industry embraces AI, entirely new roles are being created. These roles require a hybrid of finance knowledge and AI expertise, and they are likely to be some of the most important jobs in the future.

Here are a few emerging roles to consider:

- **AI/Finance Integration Specialist**: These professionals are responsible for ensuring that AI tools and financial strategies align. They may work closely with both AI development teams and finance teams to ensure the technology is being used effectively. An AI/finance integration specialist understands the intricacies of both fields and ensures that AI models are adapted to meet business goals.

- **Data Scientist (Finance)**: With a focus on the intersection of finance and data science, this role involves using machine learning and AI to analyze financial data, identify trends, and predict market outcomes. If you have a strong analytical background, learning programming languages and algorithms will position you to transition into this role.

- **Ethical AI Specialist**: As AI takes on a larger role in finance, the ethical implications of AI-driven decisions are becoming more important. Ethical AI specialists will be tasked with ensuring that AI models are transparent, fair, and free from bias. They will work to ensure that AI-driven decisions align with ethical guidelines and regulatory standards.

- **AI-Enhanced Financial Advisor**: Rather than replacing financial advisors, AI is likely to make them more efficient and effective. Financial advisors who can use AI tools to enhance their understanding of clients' portfolios, predict market movements, and optimize asset allocation will be in high demand. Advisors who can blend AI with personalized financial strategies will have a competitive advantage.

- **AI Product Manager for Finance**: With AI becoming a key technology in finance, AI product managers will play a crucial role in overseeing the development and implementation of AI tools in financial products. They will work closely with data scientists, engineers, and financial professionals to design, test, and deploy AI-powered solutions.

5. Cultivate an AI-First Mindset

To truly succeed in an AI-driven finance world, you'll need to adopt a mindset that sees AI as an asset rather than a competitor. This means being proactive in learning new technologies, seeking out new opportunities for collaboration with AI, and being willing to experiment and innovate.

- **Adopt a Growth Mindset**: Instead of fearing change, embrace it. Understand that AI is a tool that can help you do your job more efficiently and effectively. View the disruption caused by AI as an opportunity to learn, grow, and position yourself as an indispensable player in the new landscape.

- **Collaboration Over Competition**: Rather than trying to "outsmart" AI, focus on how you can collaborate with it. Look at AI as a co-worker that complements your skills and expertise. The most successful finance professionals will be those who understand how to work alongside AI to create better financial products, enhance customer experiences, and solve complex financial problems.

Conclusion: The Future Is AI-Enhanced, Not AI-Replaced

AI is transforming finance, but it's not here to replace human professionals altogether. Instead, it's providing new opportunities for those who are willing to adapt, learn, and collaborate. By upskilling, embracing new tools, and shifting your focus to strategic, high-value tasks, you can ensure your relevance in an AI-driven world.

The future of finance belongs to those who understand how to leverage AI effectively—not those who fear it. It's time to reframe AI not as a threat, but as a partner that can amplify your abilities and take your career to new heights.

Chapter 5: The New Skills You'll Need to Succeed in an AI-Driven Finance World

In the previous chapters, we've covered how AI is rapidly transforming the finance industry and why embracing these changes is essential for staying relevant in an increasingly automated world. As AI continues to take over routine tasks and automate many functions that were once the domain of human professionals, it's clear that finance professionals must adapt to new roles that emphasize higher-level thinking, strategy, and collaboration with AI systems.

In this chapter, we'll dive deep into the specific skills that will be essential for finance professionals moving forward. These are not just technical skills; they also include interpersonal and strategic skills that will enable you to thrive in a finance world where AI is not just a tool but a partner.

1. Data Literacy: The Foundation of AI-Powered Finance

At the heart of AI's ability to transform finance is its dependence on **data**. AI systems learn and make decisions based on vast amounts of data, so being able to understand, interpret, and manipulate data is a fundamental skill in the AI-powered future.

Key Data Skills to Master:

- **Data Analysis**: Finance professionals need to understand how to analyze large datasets and extract actionable insights. While AI tools can process the data, it's still crucial for you to interpret the results and apply them strategically. Knowing how to use tools like Excel, Python, R, or SQL to manipulate data will become increasingly important.

- **Data Visualization**: The ability to present data in a way that is easy to understand and actionable is invaluable. AI can generate complex reports, but it's still up to you to communicate the insights clearly to non-technical stakeholders. Learning how to use tools like Tableau, Power BI, or even advanced Excel functions to visualize data will help you deliver meaningful insights in a digestible format.

- **Understanding AI Data Models**: While you may not need to become an AI developer, you must understand the kinds of data models that AI systems use, such as supervised learning, unsupervised learning, and reinforcement learning. The ability to understand the strengths and weaknesses of these models will allow you to evaluate AI outputs and ensure they are accurate, actionable, and aligned with your financial objectives.

Example: In portfolio management, AI can sift through vast amounts of data to identify the most profitable assets. However, it's still the portfolio manager's responsibility to interpret this data, integrate it with broader market trends, and apply it to the client's overall financial strategy.

2. AI and Machine Learning Fundamentals: The Language of the Future

Understanding AI and machine learning (ML) doesn't mean you need to become a full-fledged data scientist or engineer. But having a working knowledge of the fundamentals will give you a significant edge in today's competitive finance world. AI is becoming increasingly embedded in financial services, and those who understand how it works will be best positioned to collaborate with AI tools and oversee their effectiveness.

Key AI/ML Concepts to Learn:

- **Supervised and Unsupervised Learning**: These are the two primary methods that AI systems use to "learn" from data. In supervised learning, AI is trained using labeled data (data with known outcomes), while in unsupervised learning, AI must find patterns in unlabeled data. Understanding how AI learns and the types of problems each method is best suited to will help you evaluate AI systems and adjust their use for specific financial tasks.

- **Neural Networks and Deep Learning**: These are more complex AI techniques that mimic how the human brain processes information. They are particularly useful for tasks such as pattern recognition, predictive modeling, and risk management. Understanding the basics of these models will help you communicate with data scientists and AI engineers more effectively.

- **Natural Language Processing (NLP)**: In finance, NLP is used for automating tasks like sentiment analysis (understanding market sentiment from news and social media) and parsing financial documents (such as SEC filings). Understanding how NLP algorithms work and how they are used in financial applications will be critical for roles involving AI-driven market research and reporting.

Example: A financial analyst working in risk management may need to understand the fundamentals of supervised learning to interpret AI-generated predictions regarding market downturns, so they can make decisions on mitigating risk based on the system's outputs.

3. Problem-Solving and Critical Thinking: The Human Edge

AI can analyze data, find patterns, and even predict future outcomes, but it is still far from perfect when it comes to **complex problem-solving** and **critical thinking**. AI is only as good as the data it's given and the parameters set by human experts, and it lacks the ability to understand context or address problems with a high degree of uncertainty—something that is intrinsic to the world of finance.

Why Critical Thinking Is Essential:

- **Interpretation and Context**: AI models might provide data-driven insights, but human professionals are still needed to interpret those insights within the context of broader market conditions, global economic factors, and regulatory landscapes. Critical thinking will be required to challenge AI conclusions and make nuanced judgments that align with your clients' or organization's goals.

- **Ethical Decision-Making**: AI has no inherent ethical compass. Humans will need to ensure that AI-driven decisions are ethical, transparent, and fair. As AI becomes more involved in investment and trading decisions, it will be up to finance professionals to oversee these processes and ensure that they align with ethical standards and compliance regulations.

- **Decision-Making Under Uncertainty**: Many financial decisions are made in environments full of uncertainty, such as when there are volatile market conditions, economic crises, or unpredictable geopolitical events. AI can help make predictions based on data, but it cannot predict the future with certainty. Professionals will still need to use judgment and experience to make decisions in uncertain environments.

Example: In portfolio management, while AI can optimize asset allocation, a seasoned advisor will need to weigh in when unexpected political events or market crises occur, adjusting the strategy based on experience and intuition.

4. Communication and Collaboration: The Art of AI-Human Partnership

While AI may excel in analyzing vast amounts of data and generating predictive models, it lacks the human qualities of emotional intelligence, creativity, and the ability to build relationships. As finance becomes more AI-driven, the ability to

communicate effectively and **collaborate with both AI systems and people** will become more important than ever.

Key Skills for Effective Communication and Collaboration:

- **Explaining AI Outputs**: As AI systems generate insights, finance professionals will need to interpret these outputs and explain them to stakeholders in a clear and actionable way. This requires the ability to simplify complex technical findings and make them relevant to the business or client goals.

- **Client Relationships**: AI can assist with portfolio recommendations, financial planning, and risk assessments, but it still lacks the human touch that clients expect when dealing with their financial futures. Building trust, understanding emotional cues, and offering personalized advice will remain key responsibilities for finance professionals.

- **Collaboration Across Disciplines**: Finance professionals will increasingly need to work alongside data scientists, AI engineers, and other technical experts. A finance professional who understands how to speak the "language" of AI and work alongside these teams will be more effective at ensuring AI tools are used effectively and that the insights produced align with financial objectives.

Example: A financial advisor working with AI-based investment strategies will need to explain complex algorithmic predictions in simple terms to clients, reassuring them about the potential outcomes and managing expectations in a way that an AI alone cannot.

5. Ethical and Regulatory Knowledge: Ensuring Responsible AI Use

As AI becomes a more integral part of financial decision-making, **ethical considerations** and **compliance with regulations** will be increasingly important. AI algorithms, if not monitored and tested properly, can perpetuate biases or make decisions that inadvertently discriminate against certain groups of people or violate financial regulations.

Key Ethical and Regulatory Skills:

- **Understanding AI Bias and Fairness**: Algorithms can inherit biases from the data they're trained on, leading to potentially discriminatory decisions. Finance professionals must be able to identify and address these biases, ensuring that AI systems make fair, unbiased decisions. This involves knowing how to test AI models for bias and implementing corrective measures when necessary.

- **Regulatory Compliance**: Finance professionals must ensure that AI systems adhere to regulatory standards in areas like financial reporting, trading, lending, and consumer protection. Staying up to date with changing financial regulations, such as those imposed by the SEC, GDPR, or other regulatory bodies, is essential to avoid legal pitfalls.

- **Transparency in AI Decision-Making**: As AI systems become more autonomous, it's important to understand how these systems arrive at their decisions. AI transparency and explainability are crucial in maintaining trust with clients and stakeholders. Understanding and ensuring that AI models can be "explained" in human terms will be a critical responsibility.

Example: In algorithmic trading, AI models may make decisions on buying or selling securities, but it's crucial for finance professionals to ensure that these decisions align with regulatory standards and are free from bias. This requires a deep understanding of both financial regulations and AI ethics.

Conclusion: Preparing for the AI-Enhanced Future

AI is transforming the financial industry, but this doesn't mean that human professionals are being sidelined. In fact, AI will amplify the abilities of finance professionals who are willing to **adapt, learn new skills, and collaborate with AI**. The new skill set required for success in an AI-driven finance world includes data literacy, AI/ML fundamentals, critical thinking, communication, and ethical knowledge.

By embracing AI as a tool that enhances human capabilities, finance professionals can move from being passive users of technology to active shapers of the future of finance. The skills we've discussed in this chapter will not only help you remain relevant but will position you as a leader in an AI-enhanced financial world.

In the next chapter, we'll explore how to cultivate a mindset that embraces these changes and prepares you to take full advantage of the opportunities AI presents—ensuring your long-term success in the rapidly evolving finance landscape.

Chapter 6: Building an AI-First Mindset: Thriving in a New Era of Finance

As AI continues to transform the financial landscape, it's not just the tools and technologies you need to embrace—it's also your mindset. The shift toward AI in finance isn't merely a technical or procedural change, but a **philosophical** one. The professionals who will thrive in the AI-powered future will be those who approach this transformation with a mindset of **adaptability, curiosity, and collaboration**.

In this chapter, we'll focus on how to build an **AI-first mindset**—a mindset that sees AI as an opportunity, not a threat; as a partner, not a competitor. This approach will allow you to not only survive but excel in the evolving financial ecosystem, ensuring that you remain at the cutting edge of the industry.

1. Embrace Change and Stay Adaptable

The AI revolution in finance is happening fast, and it's showing no signs of slowing down. For many finance professionals, this can be daunting. AI is disruptive—it changes the way we do business, the way we think about strategy, and even the roles we play within the organization. However, the professionals who succeed in this new world will be those who embrace **change** rather than resist it.

Key Strategies for Embracing Change:

- **Adopt a Growth Mindset**: The first step toward building an AI-first mindset is to embrace the idea that you can continuously grow, learn, and improve. Instead of fearing obsolescence, approach AI as an opportunity to **evolve**. A growth mindset allows you to see challenges as opportunities to expand your skillset and deepen your expertise. For example, if you're used to performing data analysis manually, view AI as a tool that can make your work more efficient, allowing you to focus on more strategic and value-added tasks.

- **Stay Curious**: The financial industry's relationship with AI is still in its early stages, and it's changing constantly. New applications, technologies, and trends emerge frequently. Those who succeed will be curious—constantly seeking to learn, understand, and explore the new possibilities AI brings to the table. Make it a habit to stay updated on the latest AI trends in finance. Read books, listen to podcasts, attend webinars, and take courses. The more you engage with the AI revolution, the more you'll understand its implications for your role and how you can leverage it.

- **Be Willing to Experiment**: AI isn't just about learning new tools—it's about trying new ways of working. Experimenting with different AI tools and techniques in your daily work can open up new avenues for efficiency and creativity. Whether it's automating routine tasks or using AI-powered insights to inform strategic decisions, being open to experimentation will allow you to discover innovative ways to use AI to your advantage.

Example: A risk manager might use AI to run various "what-if" scenarios and simulate future market conditions, enabling them to make more informed decisions. By embracing AI tools for predictive analytics, they can focus their energy on interpreting the results and formulating strategies rather than running manual calculations.

2. Think of AI as a Partner, Not a Competitor

One of the biggest obstacles that finance professionals face in the AI-driven world is the fear that AI will replace them. This mindset—while understandable—leads to unnecessary anxiety and resistance. The truth is that AI is not here to replace humans in finance; rather, it's here to **enhance** and **augment** human capabilities. AI is best viewed as a **partner**—a tool that can help you make smarter, faster decisions, but still requires human oversight and insight to be truly effective.

How to Shift from Competition to Collaboration with AI:

- **Recognize AI's Limitations**: AI is incredibly powerful, but it's not infallible. It operates on data, and data can be incomplete or flawed. Moreover, AI lacks human intuition, creativity, and ethical reasoning—areas where human professionals are indispensable. By understanding AI's limitations, you can better identify areas where AI can help, and where your expertise, judgment, and creativity are needed.

- **Leverage AI to Free Up Your Time**: By automating routine tasks, AI can free you from mundane, repetitive activities, allowing you to focus on higher-level strategic thinking and decision-making. For instance, AI can process transactions, analyze financial reports, or track market trends, but you can use the time AI saves you to engage with clients, build relationships, or develop creative solutions to complex problems.

- **Collaborate with AI, Not Against It**: In an AI-first world, collaboration becomes paramount. Understand how AI works and how it can be integrated into your role. This will allow you to work alongside AI as a partner rather than seeing it as something that competes for your job. Look at AI as an extra set of hands, amplifying your abilities and enabling you to focus on the tasks where human skills—such as empathy, negotiation, and strategic thinking—truly shine.

Example: A financial advisor using AI tools to recommend portfolio allocations can focus on building relationships with clients, understanding their personal goals, and making emotionally intelligent decisions, while AI handles the data-heavy work of managing risk and optimizing returns.

3. Foster a Culture of Continuous Learning

AI is evolving at a rapid pace, and the only way to stay ahead of the curve is to **commit to lifelong learning**. While this might seem overwhelming, it's important to think of learning as a process of continuous improvement rather than a one-time effort. The more you immerse yourself in the world of AI, the more you'll discover new opportunities for enhancing your work and career.

Ways to Cultivate a Learning Culture:

- **Take Ownership of Your Education**: Learning doesn't just happen in a classroom. There are countless online resources, such as MOOCs (Massive Open Online Courses), podcasts, blogs, webinars, and communities dedicated to AI in finance. Seek out these resources and make learning an ongoing habit. Identify areas where you feel less confident, such as data analytics or machine learning, and take specific steps to improve your understanding of those topics.

- **Create a Feedback Loop**: To make sure you're adapting successfully to AI tools, set up a feedback loop with colleagues, mentors, and even AI systems themselves. Ask for feedback on how you're using AI and whether there are areas for improvement. For example, you might receive feedback that a certain predictive model is giving better results with slightly different input parameters, or that certain AI recommendations can be further refined through deeper data analysis. This iterative process of learning and refining will help you stay relevant in the AI-powered finance world.

- **Learn from Others**: Join communities or networks where finance professionals share knowledge about AI applications. LinkedIn groups, professional associations, and tech forums can be great places to meet like-minded professionals, exchange ideas, and learn from those who are at the cutting edge of AI in finance.

Example: A portfolio manager could take an online course on machine learning algorithms used in financial forecasting, then apply this new knowledge to enhance their investment strategies and better understand AI's role in predicting market behavior.

4. Develop Emotional Intelligence and Ethical Awareness

While AI is transforming the technical side of finance, **human-centered skills** will continue to be essential. **Emotional intelligence (EI)**, in particular, will be a key differentiator. While AI can analyze data and make predictions, it lacks the emotional and ethical awareness required to navigate complex financial decisions—

especially those that involve clients or are fraught with social or political implications.

Why Emotional Intelligence and Ethics Matter:

- **Building Trust**: In a world where AI is increasingly involved in decision-making, clients and colleagues will need to trust that these decisions are being made transparently and ethically. A finance professional with strong emotional intelligence will be able to manage client relationships with empathy, reassure them during market volatility, and make ethical decisions that prioritize client well-being.

- **Navigating Ethical Dilemmas**: AI can optimize financial decisions based on historical data, but it might inadvertently perpetuate biases or overlook ethical concerns. A professional with strong ethical awareness will be able to guide AI applications in ways that ensure they comply with legal, regulatory, and moral standards. This is especially important in areas such as credit lending, algorithmic trading, and investment strategies, where bias or unfair decision-making can have significant consequences.

- **Human Touch in Decision-Making**: AI can provide data-driven recommendations, but it cannot empathize with a client's personal financial situation or consider non-quantifiable factors in decision-making. Finance professionals with high emotional intelligence will remain essential for offering personalized advice, understanding client needs, and making difficult decisions with human nuance.

Example: A financial planner using AI tools to optimize retirement plans for clients might still need to have a conversation with a client about their personal goals, dreams, and fears—things AI cannot understand. The human element in these decisions is irreplaceable.

5. Be a Champion of AI-Driven Innovation

As AI becomes increasingly embedded in finance, it's not enough to just adapt to changes—**you should be driving those changes**. AI presents incredible opportunities for innovation in finance, from creating new financial products to transforming customer service, risk management, and even corporate culture.

Ways to Champion AI in Your Organization:

- **Be an Advocate for AI Adoption**: As an early adopter, you can help introduce AI tools and best practices to your organization. Whether it's pitching the benefits of AI-powered risk assessment tools or advocating for AI-driven customer service chatbots, take the initiative to explore how AI can improve operations, enhance decision-making, and drive profitability.

- **Foster a Culture of Innovation**: Help your team or organization think creatively about how AI can be leveraged in new and innovative ways. This could mean developing AI-driven investment strategies, improving client interaction using AI-powered chatbots, or using machine learning to predict market trends. Encourage experimentation, cross-functional collaboration, and creative thinking.

- **Collaborate with AI Developers**: To truly unlock the potential of AI in your role, collaborate closely with data scientists and AI developers. By working together, you can identify the financial challenges AI could solve, provide valuable feedback on its implementation, and ensure that it's aligned with the organization's strategic objectives.

Example: A CFO could champion the development of an AI-powered financial forecasting tool, working closely with data scientists to tailor it to the company's unique needs, and then lead the charge in implementing it across the organization for more accurate budget predictions and cost-saving strategies.

Conclusion: Shaping the Future of Finance with AI

Building an AI-first mindset is the key to thriving in a future where AI plays a dominant role in the finance industry. By embracing change, thinking of AI as a partner, fostering continuous learning, honing emotional intelligence, and championing innovation, you'll position yourself not just as a participant in the AI revolution—but as a **leader** driving its success.

In the next chapter, we will explore how to practically apply these concepts in your day-to-day work, turning theory into actionable steps that will help you make the transition from traditional finance roles to AI-enhanced finance roles seamlessly and successfully.

Chapter 7: Practical Steps to Integrating AI into Your Daily Finance Workflow

Now that you've developed an AI-first mindset, the next step is to start **integrating AI** into your daily workflow. This is where the rubber meets the road—where the theoretical knowledge from previous chapters becomes actionable and real. It's one thing to understand the potential of AI in finance, but it's another to apply it effectively in your job.

In this chapter, we'll explore practical steps to help you seamlessly incorporate AI into your daily tasks, from automating routine processes to using AI for advanced decision-making and strategy formulation. Whether you're a financial analyst, portfolio manager, risk officer, or financial planner, AI offers tools and techniques that can radically enhance your productivity, accuracy, and decision-making abilities.

1. Automate Routine Tasks and Free Up Time for Value-Added Work

One of the most immediate benefits of AI is its ability to automate repetitive, time-consuming tasks. This can free up hours in your day, allowing you to focus on higher-value, strategic tasks that require human insight and creativity.

Key Areas to Automate:

- **Data Collection and Reporting**: Collecting data from various financial sources, inputting it into spreadsheets, and preparing reports are often tedious and prone to human error. AI can help automate these data collection processes. For example, AI can scrape financial news websites, pull data from stock exchanges, and even aggregate market sentiment from social media feeds. Tools like **Power BI**, **Tableau**, or even **Excel's AI-based tools** can automate report generation, providing up-to-date insights at the push of a button.

- **Financial Reconciliation**: AI can automate the reconciliation of financial records, cross-checking transactions, invoices, and payments against each other, ensuring consistency without manual intervention. AI-driven tools like **BlackLine** or **Trintech** help automate this process, saving hours of manual reconciliation work and reducing the risk of errors.

- **Portfolio Monitoring**: If you're a portfolio manager, AI can track the performance of various assets in real time, automatically adjusting asset allocations based on predefined parameters, market conditions, or risk tolerance. Portfolio management platforms, such as **Wealthfront** or **Betterment**, use AI to constantly evaluate portfolio performance and make recommendations for rebalancing.

Example: A financial analyst who spends a lot of time gathering data for quarterly reports could use AI-driven tools to pull financial data from multiple sources, categorize it, and even create draft reports. This would free up time for them to interpret the data and provide insights into business performance.

2. Leverage Predictive Analytics for Smarter Decision-Making

AI is a powerful tool for forecasting future trends based on historical data. Predictive analytics—powered by machine learning (ML)—is one of AI's most valuable applications in finance. By using algorithms to analyze past trends and patterns, AI can generate predictions about future market conditions, asset values, and even customer behaviors.

Key Applications of Predictive Analytics in Finance:

- **Market Forecasting**: Machine learning models can predict market trends based on historical data, interest rates, commodity prices, and even geopolitical events. Tools like **Aladdin** (BlackRock's investment management platform) use predictive analytics to model various market scenarios, allowing investment managers to make more informed decisions.

- **Credit Risk Prediction**: In lending, AI-powered models can analyze a borrower's financial history, payment patterns, and other indicators to predict their likelihood of defaulting on a loan. Credit scoring systems, such as **FICO's AI-powered model** or **Zest AI**, use machine learning to improve the accuracy of credit risk assessments.

- **Customer Churn Prediction**: For financial services companies offering subscriptions or ongoing services, AI can predict customer churn (the likelihood that a client will leave or stop using services). By analyzing patterns in transaction histories, engagement levels, and customer behavior, AI can alert teams to clients who are at risk of leaving, allowing them to take proactive steps to retain them.

- **Portfolio Optimization**: AI can help financial advisors and portfolio managers make smarter asset allocation decisions by predicting future asset returns and risk levels. **Robo-advisors** like **Wealthfront** or **Betterment** use AI to build and manage investment portfolios automatically based on individual client preferences, goals, and risk tolerance.

Example: A portfolio manager could use AI-powered tools to forecast the future performance of different sectors or companies, and then adjust their portfolio accordingly. For instance, the AI might predict a downturn in the tech sector based on macroeconomic conditions, prompting the manager to reallocate investments to more stable sectors.

3. Enhance Client Interactions and Personalization Using AI

AI can be a game-changer in client relations by enabling **personalized experiences** and **tailored financial advice**. This is particularly valuable for wealth managers, financial advisors, and institutions with a large customer base. AI tools can analyze vast amounts of data from clients, enabling financial professionals to offer highly personalized, data-driven recommendations.

How AI Enhances Client Personalization:

- **Personalized Financial Advice**: AI-powered tools, such as **Robo-advisors** or **AI-driven financial planning platforms**, can analyze a client's financial goals, risk tolerance, and investment preferences to offer personalized advice. These tools can suggest optimal investment portfolios, retirement strategies, or insurance plans based on real-time data and advanced modeling.
- **Client Communication**: AI chatbots and virtual assistants can enhance customer support by providing quick answers to

client inquiries, scheduling appointments, or offering insights into account performance. For instance, **ChatGPT** or **IBM Watson Assistant** can interact with clients, answer basic questions, and even offer investment advice based on the client's preferences.

- **Behavioral Insights**: AI can analyze client behavior patterns—such as spending, saving, and investing—and use this data to predict future needs. This allows financial advisors to anticipate when a client might need a loan, when they might be interested in investment opportunities, or when they might be considering a major life event (like retirement or home purchase).

- **Automated Reporting**: Clients often need regular reports on their portfolio performance, tax situation, or investment performance. AI-driven platforms can automatically generate personalized reports, summarizing key metrics and trends in a way that is relevant to each client's specific situation.

Example: A financial planner can use AI to track a client's spending patterns, income, and financial goals. The AI system can recommend actionable steps to meet those goals, such as reallocating their investments to achieve greater returns or adjusting their budget to increase savings.

4. Use Natural Language Processing (NLP) for Document Analysis

Natural Language Processing (NLP) is a branch of AI that focuses on understanding and interpreting human language. In finance, NLP is used to analyze large volumes of unstructured data, such as news articles, earnings calls, financial reports, and social media posts. By processing and extracting insights from this textual data, AI can provide actionable intelligence for decision-making.

Key Applications of NLP in Finance:

- **Sentiment Analysis**: NLP can analyze financial news, earnings calls, and social media to gauge market sentiment. Sentiment analysis tools can tell you whether the general sentiment towards a particular stock or sector is positive, negative, or neutral, and how this sentiment might influence market movements. Platforms like **Thomson Reuters Eikon** or **Bloomberg Terminal** leverage NLP for sentiment analysis in real-time, helping traders and investors make faster decisions.

- **Automated Document Review**: For financial institutions, reviewing contracts, loan documents, or financial statements can be time-consuming. AI-driven NLP models can analyze and extract relevant information from these documents, streamlining the due diligence process. AI-powered platforms like **Kira Systems** or **LawGeex** are used for contract analysis in legal and financial services, saving time and reducing errors.

- **Earnings Call Transcripts**: Investors can use NLP to scan earnings call transcripts for specific keywords, trends, or statements that might indicate future company performance. AI tools can flag important segments of the transcript, helping analysts to quickly focus on the most critical information.

- **Regulatory Compliance**: For financial professionals, staying compliant with regulations is paramount. AI-powered NLP tools can scan regulatory documents and legal texts, automatically identifying relevant rules and ensuring that the organization is staying compliant.

Example: A wealth management firm could use NLP to scan earnings call transcripts from companies in their client's portfolios, flagging positive or negative language that might impact stock performance. This would allow the firm to react faster than manual review.

5. Implement AI for Risk Management and Fraud Detection

AI is also revolutionizing how financial institutions approach **risk management** and **fraud detection**. By analyzing vast datasets in real-time, AI systems can identify potential risks and fraudulent activities much faster and more accurately than traditional methods.

How AI Improves Risk Management:

- **Credit Risk Modeling**: AI can analyze client data, transaction history, and even social behavior to predict the likelihood of default. This improves credit risk assessments and allows for more informed decision-making in loan approvals. **Zest AI** and **Upstart** are examples of platforms using AI to enhance credit risk models.

- **Fraud Detection**: AI systems are adept at detecting unusual patterns in transaction data that may indicate fraudulent activity. Machine learning models can analyze thousands of transactions per second and flag suspicious behavior based on historical trends, helping banks and financial institutions stop fraud before it occurs. Companies like **Darktrace** and **Kount** use AI for real-time fraud detection.

- **Market Risk Assessment**: AI tools can assess market risks by analyzing complex datasets, including market conditions, economic indicators, and social sentiment. These tools can provide early warnings about potential market shifts, enabling finance professionals to adjust strategies before major risks materialize.

Example: A bank could use AI-powered fraud detection software to flag unusual customer behavior—such as a sudden large withdrawal or rapid international transfers—that could indicate identity theft or account fraud. The AI would raise alerts in real-time, allowing the bank to intervene and prevent loss.

Conclusion: Turning AI into Action

Integrating AI into your daily finance workflow requires both **understanding its potential** and **knowing how to use it** to drive meaningful outcomes. From automating repetitive tasks to using predictive analytics for smarter decision-making, AI can streamline your work, enhance your insights, and help you stay ahead in the fast-changing finance world.

The practical steps outlined in this chapter are just the beginning. As you continue to experiment with AI, you'll discover new ways to leverage it for personal and organizational success. The key is to stay curious, continuously learn, and be open to exploring innovative applications of AI that can elevate your work in finance.

In the next chapter, we'll explore how to **future-proof your career** by developing advanced AI skills and positioning yourself as a leader in the AI-driven financial world.

Chapter 8: Future-Proofing Your Career in an AI-Driven Finance World

As AI continues to reshape the finance industry, it's crucial to think not just about how you can adapt today, but how you can **future-proof your career** for the long term. AI is already a game-changer, and its influence is only set to expand in the coming years. The most successful finance professionals will be those who not only embrace AI as a tool but actively **build new skills, develop leadership qualities, and stay ahead of the curve** in an ever-changing landscape.

In this chapter, we will explore how you can equip yourself with the **skills**, **mindset**, and **strategies** necessary to thrive in the AI-powered finance world. Whether you're an entry-level analyst or a seasoned executive, the principles of career resilience and forward-thinking innovation will apply. Let's break down the steps you can take to ensure that you remain indispensable, relevant, and ahead of the competition.

1. Developing Advanced AI Skills and Knowledge

AI is no longer the domain of data scientists and engineers alone. As a finance professional, you need to **actively develop an understanding of AI technologies** to remain competitive and take full advantage of their potential. While you don't need to become a machine learning expert, gaining a solid understanding of key concepts and practical applications will set you apart.

Key Skills to Develop:

- **Data Literacy**: In an AI-driven world, **data is king**, and understanding how to work with it is critical. Familiarize yourself with basic **data analysis** techniques, such as **data cleaning**, **data visualization**, and **data interpretation**. Learning how to extract insights from large datasets will become one of your most valuable skills. Tools like **Excel**, **Tableau**, **Power BI**, and **Google Data Studio** are essential for this.

- **Machine Learning (ML) Fundamentals**: While you don't need to build models from scratch, understanding the basics of machine learning will help you collaborate more effectively with data scientists and developers. Start by learning about supervised vs. unsupervised learning, regression analysis, decision trees, clustering, and neural networks. There are many online resources, such as **Coursera**, **edX**, and **Kaggle**, that offer beginner-friendly courses in ML for finance professionals.

- **AI Tools and Platforms**: Familiarize yourself with AI-powered platforms and tools that are widely used in finance.

For instance, platforms like **Aladdin** (BlackRock), **Kensho**, and **Numerai** provide AI-driven analytics and financial forecasting. Understanding how these tools work and how they can be applied in your job will help you maximize their benefits. Some companies also offer their own proprietary AI tools, which you should seek to learn in-depth if they're integral to your organization.

- **Programming Languages**: While not strictly necessary for all finance professionals, learning **Python** or **R** can be incredibly useful. These programming languages are the backbone of many AI and machine learning models. With Python, you can access **pandas** (for data analysis), **matplotlib** (for visualization), and **scikit-learn** (for machine learning) — all of which are widely used in finance.

- **AI Ethics and Governance**: As AI becomes more integrated into financial decision-making, understanding **AI ethics**, fairness, transparency, and governance will be crucial. Study topics like bias in AI, algorithmic accountability, and data privacy. Being able to navigate the **ethical landscape** of AI will not only enhance your credibility but also prepare you for roles in **AI compliance** or **risk management**.

Example: A financial analyst who has a basic understanding of machine learning can work with a data scientist to create custom models that predict stock market trends based on historical price data, economic indicators, and social media sentiment. This collaboration can lead to more accurate and actionable insights.

2. Cultivating Strategic Thinking and Leadership Qualities

AI is more than just a tool for improving operational efficiency—it's a strategic enabler that can transform business models and market positioning. The future of finance will be led by professionals who can think strategically about how to leverage AI in both day-to-day operations and long-term growth. Developing **leadership qualities** will be essential as AI continues to alter the dynamics of the finance industry.

Key Areas to Focus On:

- **Strategic Vision**: As AI continues to transform the industry, it's important to develop the ability to **see the big picture**. Understand how AI fits into broader financial trends such as digital transformation, **fintech innovation**, and **regulatory changes**. This strategic vision will help you anticipate market shifts and create AI-powered strategies that give your company a competitive edge.

- **Project Management Skills**: With AI projects becoming more common, **project management** skills will be essential for leading or overseeing AI initiatives. Familiarize yourself with **Agile methodologies**, **Scrum**, and other project management frameworks that are commonly used in AI and technology development. Being able to manage AI-driven projects, work cross-functionally, and ensure timely delivery will be crucial in AI adoption.

- **Collaboration with Cross-Functional Teams**: In the AI-powered finance landscape, you'll be working alongside data scientists, engineers, and technology teams. Building your **collaboration and communication skills** will allow you to effectively bridge the gap between business and technical teams. Financial professionals with the ability to speak both the language of finance and technology will be highly sought after.

- **Executive Leadership**: As finance professionals ascend to leadership roles, they will need to drive the organization's AI strategy. Understanding the ethical, regulatory, and societal implications of AI, as well as how AI fits into overall business strategies, will be key in executive decision-making. Start developing leadership capabilities in areas such as change management, innovation management, and AI ethics, as these will be increasingly important at the C-suite level.

Example: A senior financial manager leading an AI implementation project in their company might oversee the creation of an AI-powered financial forecasting model. Their role isn't just to ensure the model is functional but also to strategize on how the model can align with broader corporate goals, such as **cost reduction**, **market expansion**, or **customer engagement**.

3. Building an AI-Enabled Network and Personal Brand

As AI reshapes finance, **networking** and **personal branding** will be essential for advancing your career. Building relationships with industry peers, staying engaged with the latest AI developments, and positioning yourself as an AI-savvy professional will help you navigate the future of finance.

Key Strategies for Networking and Branding:

- **Engage with AI Communities**: Join professional associations, forums, and online communities where finance professionals and AI experts discuss industry trends and best practices. For example, you can join AI-focused groups on LinkedIn, participate in webinars hosted by organizations like the **Global Association of Risk Professionals (GARP)**, or attend AI-specific finance conferences like **FinTech Connect**.

- **Build Your Thought Leadership**: Share your insights and experiences with AI in finance through blog posts, articles, or even social media. Engaging in conversations around AI ethics, AI-driven investment strategies, and AI tools will establish you as a **thought leader** in your field. Start small by contributing to industry publications or your company's blog.

- **Mentorship and Collaboration**: Connect with mentors who are experts in AI and finance, and be open to mentoring others who are just beginning to understand AI. This will not only deepen your knowledge but also help you stay connected with the pulse of the industry. Consider collaborating with colleagues in data science or AI research departments to build interdisciplinary knowledge.

- **Stay Visible in AI-Focused Networks**: Attend AI-focused conferences, hackathons, or roundtables where you can meet people who are leading the way in AI adoption within finance. By staying engaged with these events, you'll not only learn about new AI tools and trends but also keep your **professional profile** visible to key decision-makers in the industry.

Example: A risk officer at a large bank can enhance their personal brand by writing articles or participating in panels discussing the ethical implications of AI in risk management. By consistently sharing relevant insights, they can establish themselves as a leading voice in the AI-powered risk management community.

4. Emphasizing Adaptability and Lifelong Learning

The finance world is changing so rapidly that the skills you learn today may not be enough tomorrow. To future-proof your career, you need to embrace **lifelong learning** and stay adaptable in an AI-driven world.

How to Foster Lifelong Learning:

- **Take Continuous Courses**: AI and technology evolve quickly. Stay ahead by continuously taking online courses, attending workshops, and reading research papers. Platforms like **Coursera**, **Udemy**, and **Kaggle** offer specialized courses in AI, machine learning, and finance.

- **Cross-Train in Other Disciplines**: Diversify your skillset by learning about complementary fields such as **data science**, **blockchain technology**, **cybersecurity**, and **regulation**. The more cross-disciplinary knowledge you have, the better you will be able to integrate AI into your specific finance role.

- **Adapt to New Technologies**: When new tools or platforms emerge, take the initiative to learn about them. Experiment with AI-driven finance tools on your own, ask your company to invest in training, and encourage innovation within your team. The more adaptable you are, the more valuable you will be to your organization.

Example: A financial advisor who continually updates their skills in both AI and behavioral finance may learn how to use AI-driven tools to better understand client psychology, potentially developing a more personalized, data-driven client approach.

5. Staying Ahead of Ethical and Regulatory Challenges in AI

As AI becomes more integrated into finance, there will be increased scrutiny on how AI is used, especially regarding **ethical concerns** and **regulatory compliance**. Professionals who can navigate these challenges will be better positioned for leadership roles.

Key Areas to Focus On:

- **AI Ethics and Bias Mitigation**: Understanding how AI can inadvertently reinforce biases and taking steps to mitigate these biases will be critical. Stay informed about the latest AI fairness frameworks and best practices for **ethical AI**. This will help ensure that AI applications are both effective and aligned with regulatory standards.

- **Regulatory Compliance**: With financial regulations evolving rapidly, understanding the intersection of AI and regulatory compliance is essential. This includes being aware of data protection laws, such as **GDPR** in the EU, and AI-specific regulations that may arise, such as the **AI Act** in the EU.

Example: A compliance officer working with AI-powered trading systems may ensure that the algorithms comply with the latest regulatory guidelines, ensuring transparency and accountability in automated decision-making processes.

Conclusion: Ready for the AI-Powered Future of Finance

The future of finance will be defined by those who embrace AI, upskill continuously, and strategically lead the charge in implementing AI solutions across the business. By developing advanced AI skills, cultivating leadership qualities, and staying adaptable, you'll not only secure your place in the evolving finance landscape but position yourself as a leader driving innovation and transformation.

As you begin to apply these strategies, remember that the most successful professionals are those who are **always learning, always adapting**, and **always thinking ahead**. The next chapter will focus on **how to take your AI-enhanced role to the next level**, including advanced strategies for leading AI initiatives within your organization.

Chapter 9: Leading AI Initiatives in Your Organization: From Strategy to Execution

As AI becomes an integral part of the financial landscape, it's no longer enough for professionals to simply **adapt** or **incorporate** AI into their work. The real opportunity lies in **leading AI initiatives** within your organization—becoming a change agent who drives AI adoption and maximizes its potential across business units. Whether you're a senior executive, department head, or emerging leader, leading AI initiatives requires a combination of strategic vision, technical understanding, and effective execution.

In this chapter, we'll explore how you can transition from an AI adopter to an AI leader within your organization. We'll focus on **how to champion AI projects, align AI strategy with organizational goals, build cross-functional teams**, and **measure the success** of your AI initiatives. These steps will enable you to **take ownership** of AI transformation efforts and establish yourself as a driving force in the future of finance.

1. Establishing a Clear AI Vision and Strategy

AI is not a one-size-fits-all solution. To lead AI initiatives effectively, you must first understand **how AI can align with and amplify your organization's strategic goals**. Successful AI adoption begins with **setting a clear vision** that articulates how AI will create value for the company and its stakeholders.

Key Steps to Establishing an AI Strategy:

- **Identify Core Business Challenges**: Start by identifying the **core challenges** your organization is facing that AI can help solve. These could be anything from streamlining operations, improving decision-making accuracy, mitigating risks, enhancing customer experience, or boosting profitability. As a leader, your job is to connect AI initiatives to specific business outcomes.

    - For example, if your company is facing inefficiencies in financial forecasting, an AI-driven solution like machine learning-powered predictive models could help streamline the process and improve accuracy.

- **Align AI Goals with Business Objectives**: Ensure that AI initiatives are aligned with your organization's **business objectives**. Whether it's improving cost-efficiency, driving revenue growth, or enhancing customer satisfaction, AI projects should serve the company's overarching vision. Clear goals ensure that AI initiatives contribute to the company's growth and not just for the sake of implementing technology.

- **Define Key Performance Indicators (KPIs)**: Setting clear, measurable KPIs will help you evaluate the success of your AI initiatives. Some common AI-specific KPIs include:

    - **Increased operational efficiency** (e.g., reducing time spent on manual tasks)

    - **Cost savings** (e.g., reducing overhead by automating processes)

    - **Revenue growth** (e.g., by using AI for personalized customer insights and cross-selling)

    - **Accuracy improvements** (e.g., enhancing predictive modeling or risk assessments)

    - **Customer satisfaction** (e.g., through AI-enhanced customer service tools)

- **Anticipate Challenges and Risks**: A key part of AI strategy is being proactive about potential challenges such as **data quality issues**, **lack of talent**, **employee resistance**, and **regulatory concerns**. Addressing these obstacles upfront will help create smoother implementation.

Example: A CFO at a large corporation may decide to implement AI for financial forecasting, aligning the AI strategy with goals of improving budget accuracy and driving cost savings. By setting KPIs such as improving forecast accuracy by 15% or reducing time spent on manual data entry by 30%, the CFO can measure the success of the initiative.

2. Building a Cross-Functional AI Team

AI projects rarely succeed in silos. They require collaboration between departments with diverse expertise. To lead a successful AI initiative, you'll need to build a **cross-functional team** that can bring together business, technical, and regulatory knowledge to ensure comprehensive AI solutions.

Essential Roles in a Cross-Functional AI Team:

- **AI/ML Engineers and Data Scientists**: These professionals will develop, train, and deploy the AI models. They have the technical expertise to ensure the models work as intended, and their job is to transform business needs into actionable algorithms and data processes.

- **Finance and Business Experts**: These are the professionals who understand the company's financial, operational, and strategic goals. Your role as a finance leader is crucial because you need to bridge the gap between the technical team and the business side of things. You'll be the one articulating the value of AI in terms that resonate with stakeholders.

- **Data Engineers**: These specialists are responsible for **data infrastructure**—ensuring the data is available, clean, and structured for AI applications. They build the data pipelines that ensure smooth data flow across departments.

- **Product Managers**: Product managers help coordinate AI development across teams, ensuring that the project is aligned with user needs, company goals, and timelines.

- **Compliance and Legal Experts**: AI initiatives, particularly in finance, are subject to various legal and regulatory requirements. Having compliance experts who understand data privacy, security laws (such as GDPR), and AI ethics is critical to ensure AI initiatives are legally sound.

- **Change Management Experts**: AI adoption often faces resistance, especially if it threatens job security or established workflows. Change management professionals can help ensure a smooth transition, fostering a culture of innovation while addressing employee concerns.

Example: A financial institution looking to implement AI in its risk management process might form a team consisting of data scientists (to build risk assessment models), business analysts (to translate the risk model into actionable insights), compliance officers (to ensure data security and regulatory compliance), and a project manager to coordinate the efforts across teams.

3. Driving AI Adoption Across the Organization

Even with a clear strategy and a well-rounded team, one of the biggest hurdles to AI implementation is ensuring **buy-in** from stakeholders and getting the entire organization on board. AI adoption is a **cultural shift** that requires significant change management.

Steps to Drive AI Adoption:

- **Communicate the Value of AI**: AI may seem abstract or intimidating to some employees, especially those without a technical background. As a leader, it's crucial to **communicate the practical benefits** of AI in terms that employees can understand. Use case studies, examples from other industries, and clear explanations of how AI can make their jobs easier or more efficient.

- **Start with Pilot Projects**: Rather than attempting a large-scale rollout immediately, begin with **pilot projects** that address a specific problem or opportunity. This allows you to test AI's impact on a smaller scale, demonstrate its potential, and address any issues before scaling up.

- **Training and Upskilling**: As AI is integrated into the organization, employees may feel the need to upgrade their skills. Offering **training programs** and resources on AI fundamentals, data literacy, and how to work with AI tools will help reduce resistance and boost confidence in the new technology.

- **Addressing Fears and Concerns**: Some employees might fear that AI will replace their jobs. It's essential to frame AI as a **tool** that enhances human decision-making and productivity rather than as a replacement for workers. **Emphasize that AI is meant to free up employees to focus on more creative and strategic tasks**. Create transparency around how AI will change workflows and what support will be provided.

- **Building a Culture of Innovation**: AI adoption thrives in environments that encourage experimentation and **continuous learning**. Create a safe space where employees can experiment with AI tools, share their feedback, and suggest new ways AI can be used. This openness will not only improve AI initiatives but will foster a culture of innovation across the organization.

Example: A bank implementing an AI-driven chat service for customer support might start by introducing the technology to a small group of agents. They can receive training on how to use the chatbot alongside their own work, gradually building confidence and demonstrating how AI frees up time for more complex customer inquiries.

4. Measuring and Scaling AI Initiatives

Once your AI initiative is live, it's critical to monitor its effectiveness and scale successful solutions across the organization. **Measuring success** and iterating based on insights is essential to maximizing the value of your AI investment.

Key Steps to Measure AI Success:

- **Track KPIs**: Evaluate the impact of your AI initiatives using the KPIs you set at the beginning of the project. For example, if your AI model is designed to improve financial forecasting, assess whether it has increased the accuracy of forecasts or reduced the time required to generate them.

- **Continuous Improvement**: AI systems need to be constantly monitored and updated. Regularly review the performance of AI models and assess whether they need fine-tuning based on new data, shifting business objectives, or changing market conditions.

- **Feedback Loops**: Implement feedback loops from all stakeholders—especially end-users who are interacting with the AI. Gathering **feedback** from business users, clients, and employees will help you identify areas for improvement.

- **Scalability**: If a pilot AI project proves successful, plan for scaling it to other parts of the organization. For instance, if an AI model that predicts cash flow is successful in one department, it can be adapted for use across other departments, leading to broader financial benefits.

- **Return on Investment (ROI)**: Track the financial benefits AI brings to the company. These can include cost reductions, improved accuracy, faster decision-making, and increased revenues. **AI ROI** should be evaluated over time as the technology matures and is integrated more deeply into business operations.

Example: After implementing an AI-driven fraud detection system, a bank tracks the number of fraudulent transactions detected and prevented, compares the results with traditional methods, and calculates the reduction in fraud-related losses. If the AI model demonstrates significant improvement, the bank can scale it to more transaction types or regions.

5. Leading Ethical AI Initiatives

AI implementation in finance comes with significant **ethical responsibilities**. As a leader, you must ensure that your AI projects uphold principles of fairness, transparency, and accountability. This involves being proactive about the ethical implications of AI and taking steps to ensure the technology is used responsibly.

Key Steps for Ethical AI Leadership:

- **Establish AI Governance Frameworks**: Develop internal **AI governance** protocols that ensure AI models are transparent, explainable, and fair. This framework should also monitor AI for any unintended consequences, such as bias or discriminatory outcomes.

- **Bias Mitigation**: Regularly audit your AI models to detect and mitigate **biases** that could affect decision-making. This is especially critical in financial services where biased models can lead to unfair lending, insurance pricing, or hiring practices.

- **Regulatory Compliance**: Stay abreast of evolving regulations and ensure your AI solutions comply with relevant laws, such as the **GDPR** or **AI ethics laws** that may be introduced. Establishing a compliance framework for AI can help prevent regulatory issues.

Example: A fintech company using AI to determine loan eligibility can mitigate bias by implementing regular audits of the algorithm and ensuring that the training data is representative of all demographic groups. An AI governance committee might be established to oversee the ethical application of AI models.

Conclusion: Becoming an AI Leader in Finance

Leading AI initiatives requires not only a technical understanding of the technology but also the ability to drive strategic change, manage cross-functional teams, and prioritize ethical considerations. By following the steps outlined in this chapter—**from establishing a clear AI vision to measuring success and ensuring ethical practices**—you can position yourself as a leader in your organization's AI transformation journey.

As AI continues to reshape the finance industry, your ability to lead AI initiatives will define your career trajectory. The key is to stay informed, remain adaptable, and actively drive AI innovation with a vision for long-term success. In the next chapter, we'll explore how to **build a sustainable career** in AI and finance, ensuring that your leadership continues to grow alongside the rapidly advancing field.

Chapter 10: Building a Sustainable Career in AI and Finance: Preparing for the Future

As AI becomes increasingly integrated into finance, it's clear that the future belongs to those who can **combine deep financial expertise** with **advanced technological skills**. However, it's not enough to simply be adept at working with AI tools or leading AI projects. To truly future-proof your career, you need to focus on **building a sustainable career path** that not only adapts to AI innovations but thrives because of them.

In this chapter, we will explore how you can **stay relevant in an AI-driven world, continually grow your skills, develop long-term career strategies**, and **maintain your professional resilience** in the face of change. We'll also look at how you can position yourself for leadership opportunities in the evolving landscape of finance and AI.

1. Understanding the Long-Term Trends Shaping AI in Finance

To build a sustainable career in AI and finance, you first need to **understand the macro trends** that are shaping the industry. These trends will not only influence the type of AI technologies emerging but also the kinds of roles and opportunities that will be available in the future.

Key Trends to Watch:

- **Continued AI Democratization**: AI tools are becoming more accessible and user-friendly, which means that AI isn't just for data scientists and engineers anymore. Financial professionals at all levels will be expected to engage with AI in a variety of ways. This trend towards democratization will make AI more ubiquitous in finance and will require finance professionals to continually upskill to stay competitive.

- **AI and Regulation**: As AI becomes more pervasive, there will be increasing scrutiny from regulators. **Financial regulations**—such as the **GDPR** in Europe or the **AI Act**—are likely to evolve rapidly, ensuring transparency, fairness, and accountability in AI applications. This will open up career opportunities in **AI governance**, **compliance**, and **risk management** within financial organizations.

- **Ethical AI**: AI ethics is an emerging field that will become more central to finance. As financial institutions use AI to make high-stakes decisions (e.g., credit scoring, insurance underwriting, investment strategies), ensuring that AI systems are fair, unbiased, and transparent will be critical. Finance professionals with expertise in **ethical AI**, **algorithmic fairness**, and **data privacy** will be in high demand.

- **AI in FinTech and DeFi**: The rise of **FinTech** (financial technology) and **Decentralized Finance (DeFi)** is rapidly transforming the financial ecosystem. AI is integral to the success of many FinTech innovations, such as **automated** trading platforms, robo-advisors, and blockchain technologies. A career path that explores the intersection of AI, blockchain, and DeFi can offer long-term growth opportunities.

- **Human-AI Collaboration**: AI will not replace human professionals in finance; instead, it will augment their abilities. The future of finance will involve **human-AI collaboration**, where financial professionals focus on high-value activities—such as strategy, judgment, and client relationships—while AI handles data-heavy tasks like analysis, forecasting, and fraud detection. Building a career that embraces this synergy will help you maintain relevance in the industry.

Example: A financial professional who is well-versed in AI technologies, data privacy regulations, and ethical frameworks might pursue a career in **AI governance** or **compliance**, ensuring that AI-driven financial services adhere to regulatory standards and ethical guidelines.

2. Continuous Learning: Keeping Your Skills Relevant

As the financial world continues to integrate AI, the most important thing you can do to future-proof your career is **commit to lifelong learning**. The pace of technological change means that the skills you acquire today may need to be upgraded tomorrow. Staying ahead of these changes and maintaining your competitive edge requires intentional effort.

Key Strategies for Continuous Learning:

- **Stay Updated on AI Developments**: Follow industry news, blogs, and thought leaders to keep up with the latest developments in AI and finance. Websites like **TechCrunch**, **Wired**, **The Financial Times**, and **Artificial Intelligence**

Finance offer valuable insights into new AI tools, regulatory changes, and emerging trends in finance.
- **Participate in Online Courses and Certifications**: There are countless resources available online to help you upgrade your skills in AI and finance. Many of these platforms offer specialized certifications that can boost your credibility. Some popular platforms include:

    - **Coursera**, **edX**, **Udemy**, and **LinkedIn Learning** for AI and finance courses.

    - **AI certifications** from organizations like **Google AI** and **IBM** can help you deepen your understanding of machine learning, data analytics, and ethical AI.

    - Financial certifications like the **CFA** (Chartered Financial Analyst) or **FRM** (Financial Risk Manager) now include modules on AI and machine learning, adding an edge to your traditional financial expertise.

- **Engage in Hands-on Projects**: Theory alone won't give you the real-world expertise you need. Get involved in projects that integrate AI into financial processes. This could mean working with your organization's data science team to implement AI models, building your own projects using publicly available data, or participating in hackathons or open-source AI projects to gain hands-on experience.

- **Develop Data-Driven Thinking**: The future of finance is data-driven, so strengthening your **data literacy** is critical. You don't need to become a data scientist, but developing the ability to **interpret data**, **identify trends**, and **extract actionable insights** will be an invaluable skill. Learn tools like **SQL**, **Python**, **R**, and **Tableau** that can help you manipulate and analyze data.

- **Cross-Train in Emerging Technologies**: As AI is often integrated with other advanced technologies, **cross-training** in fields like **blockchain**, **cloud computing**, and

cybersecurity can position you as a more well-rounded professional. For example, understanding how AI works with blockchain technology could position you as an expert in **AI-powered decentralized finance (DeFi)** solutions.

Example: A financial planner might learn how AI-driven robo-advisors are reshaping wealth management by completing online courses in **algorithmic trading** and **financial modeling**. By staying ahead of these changes, they can enhance their services and differentiate themselves in the marketplace.

3. Building a Personal Brand and Network

In an AI-driven finance world, your **personal brand** and **professional network** can make all the difference in your career trajectory. Building a reputation as someone who understands both finance and AI, and who can contribute meaningfully to conversations about the future of the industry, will help you unlock new opportunities.

Key Steps to Build Your Personal Brand and Network:

- **Share Your Expertise**: Start sharing your insights and expertise about AI and finance. This can be done through blogging, speaking at industry events, or publishing articles on platforms like **Medium**, **LinkedIn**, or **Finextra**. Sharing your thought leadership helps establish you as a credible professional and attracts opportunities.

- **Engage in Industry Groups and Communities**: Join professional organizations like the **Global Association of Risk Professionals (GARP)**, **CFA Institute**, or **Financial Planning Association (FPA)**, which are increasingly focusing on AI and technology in finance. These groups offer great networking opportunities, conferences, and workshops where you can stay ahead of industry trends.

- **Network with AI and Tech Experts**: AI in finance is a highly interdisciplinary field, and it's important to network with experts outside of the traditional finance realm. Attend AI-focused conferences (e.g., **AI in Finance Summit, AI Expo Global**), workshops, and webinars, where you can learn from industry leaders and engage in cross-disciplinary discussions.

- **Seek Mentorship and Provide Mentorship**: Find mentors who have already successfully navigated the intersection of AI and finance. Having someone to guide you through the complexities of this evolving field will be invaluable. Conversely, offering mentorship to newcomers can help you stay sharp and can position you as a leader in the field.

- **Develop a Digital Presence**: In today's connected world, having an active **digital presence** is essential. Keep your LinkedIn profile updated with your accomplishments, share your learning journey, and contribute to discussions about AI's role in the future of finance. Participate in relevant Twitter discussions, or publish your thoughts on **LinkedIn Pulse** or **Medium**.

Example: A senior financial strategist who regularly shares insights on AI's role in shaping market predictions might attract the attention of recruiters or collaborators looking to innovate in financial analytics. Their thought leadership could also lead to speaking opportunities at fintech events.

4. Navigating Career Transitions in an AI-Driven Environment

AI will continue to reshape not just how finance professionals do their jobs, but the types of roles that exist within the industry. Some traditional roles may become obsolete, while others will evolve or emerge entirely. It's crucial to be open to **career transitions** and agile enough to pivot as new opportunities arise.

How to Navigate Career Transitions:

- **Stay Agile and Open to Change**: Don't be afraid to pivot your career if the landscape shifts. For example, if you have a strong background in financial modeling, you might transition into a role focused on developing or managing AI models for financial forecasting.

- **Look for New Roles in AI and Finance**: As AI continues to influence the finance industry, new roles will emerge that didn't exist just a few years ago. Positions like **AI Strategy Officer, AI Data Steward, Financial Data Scientist**, or **AI Ethics Consultant** may become increasingly common. Stay on the lookout for new roles where AI and finance intersect.

- **Upskill in Specialized Areas**: As financial markets become more data-driven, **specialized roles** such as **quantitative analyst (quant), data engineer**, or **AI financial risk manager** will be in high demand. Stay focused on acquiring the technical skills that will allow you to transition smoothly into these more specialized roles.

- **Invest in Emotional Intelligence (EQ)**: While AI can handle complex data-driven tasks, it's the human element—**empathy, judgment, creativity**, and **interpersonal skills**—that AI can't replicate. Continue developing your emotional intelligence and interpersonal skills to thrive in roles that require human decision-making and leadership.

Example: A financial analyst working with spreadsheets and reports might transition into a role as an **AI financial data strategist**, using advanced AI tools to analyze large datasets, or even shift into a more client-facing role where they guide clients through AI-powered investment strategies.

Conclusion: Becoming a Resilient AI-Finance Leader

The future of finance will be defined by **those who can innovate** with AI, adapt to technological disruptions, and continuously learn and grow. By understanding AI's potential, focusing on lifelong learning, building a strong network, and staying agile, you can create a **sustainable career** that not only survives but thrives in the AI-powered future of finance.

As the industry evolves, the most successful professionals will be those who see change as an opportunity, not a threat—those who embrace AI, collaborate with technology, and continuously upskill to stay relevant. Your ability to integrate **AI with financial expertise** will be a key differentiator, ensuring that your career remains both fulfilling and future-proof.

In the next chapter, we will explore **how to transition from being an AI-augmented professional to an AI-driven leader**, taking charge of AI adoption and transformation within your organization, and leading your team toward success in an AI-driven world.

Chapter 11: AI Tools vs. Human Performance: Achieving Superior Risk-Adjusted Returns

One of the most compelling reasons for the financial industry's increasing adoption of AI tools is the ability to **optimize risk-adjusted returns**—a metric that is crucial for investors, portfolio managers, and financial institutions. The primary advantage of AI in this context lies in its ability to process vast amounts of data, identify patterns, and make decisions at speeds and accuracies far beyond human capabilities. While human financial professionals rely on intuition, experience, and historical data, AI leverages **real-time data processing, machine learning**, and **predictive algorithms** to enhance decision-making and risk management.

This chapter will explore how **AI tools** can surpass human performance in managing risk-adjusted returns, focusing on several key factors, including:

- **Data processing capabilities**: AI's ability to analyze vast datasets far beyond human capacity.

- **Predictive power**: AI's ability to forecast returns and volatility more accurately than traditional methods.

- **Behavioral bias mitigation**: How AI helps eliminate the psychological biases that often lead human investors astray.

- **Performance evidence**: Real-world examples and studies showing how AI tools have delivered superior risk-adjusted returns.

We will also discuss how the combination of **AI-driven insights** and human expertise could reshape the future of investment management, leading to more **efficient markets** and potentially higher returns.

1. AI's Advantage in Data Processing and Speed

AI tools can process vast amounts of data in real-time, allowing them to make decisions based on **far more variables** than a human could ever analyze manually. Financial markets are increasingly data-driven, and as the volume and complexity of data continue to increase, AI's superior ability to process this data becomes a clear advantage.

AI in Quantitative Analysis and High-Frequency Trading (HFT)
In **high-frequency trading (HFT)**, AI algorithms can analyze market data and execute trades in microseconds—far faster than human traders can react. These AI models aren't just looking at prices; they're analyzing **market depth**, **order book flow**, **news**

sentiment, **macroeconomic data**, and even social media feeds in real-time. This kind of data processing allows AI systems to identify **small price discrepancies** that are too fleeting for humans to capitalize on. AI can take advantage of **millisecond-level trading windows**, generating profits based on predictive signals that humans would miss.

Example: The AI-powered trading platform **Renaissance Technologies**, a leader in quantitative hedge funds, has delivered remarkable returns by using advanced algorithms to process enormous datasets and adjust trading strategies on the fly. According to research by **The Financial Times**, Renaissance's **Medallion Fund** has produced annual returns of around **35%** net of fees over the past 30 years—far outpacing human-managed funds.

Data Source:

- "The Hidden Genius of Renaissance Technologies' Medallion Fund," **Financial Times**, 2020.

AI's data processing capabilities also extend to broader market analysis. While a human analyst might focus on **macroeconomic indicators** or **corporate earnings reports**, an AI tool can analyze thousands of data points, including **geopolitical risks**, **consumer sentiment**, and **environmental factors**, and weigh them in real-time to adjust portfolio allocations. This can result in a more **dynamic, adaptive strategy** that continually optimizes for **risk-adjusted returns**.

2. Enhanced Predictive Capabilities and Forecasting Accuracy

The ability to predict asset prices, volatility, and risk factors is critical for optimizing **risk-adjusted returns**. Traditional investment strategies rely on **historical data** to make forecasts, but human analysts can only process so much information at a time, often relying on simplified models and assumptions. AI, on the other hand, can apply advanced **machine learning algorithms** to detect non-obvious patterns in vast datasets, improving the accuracy of predictions.

Machine Learning in Predicting Market Movements
AI tools, especially **deep learning** and **reinforcement learning**, can learn from historical market data and continuously adapt to new information. They don't just look at a single asset or a single indicator; they take into account **interrelationships** across a wide range of financial variables. For instance, an AI model might combine **corporate earnings**, **interest rate changes**, **global trade tensions**, and **commodity price fluctuations** to make more informed predictions about an asset's future price movements.

Example: A study by **J.P. Morgan** demonstrated that AI models could predict market volatility with higher precision than traditional methods. In one experiment, a deep learning model outperformed human analysts in predicting the **VIX (volatility index)**, an important indicator of market risk. By incorporating diverse data sources and adjusting for real-time changes, AI improved forecasting accuracy, leading to better risk management and enhanced returns.

Data Source:

- "Artificial Intelligence in Financial Markets," **J.P. Morgan**, 2021.

Forecasting Volatility and Managing Risk
AI tools are particularly adept at managing **volatility**, a key factor in risk-adjusted returns. Volatility forecasting typically involves complex statistical models that predict how much an asset's price is likely to fluctuate. While human analysts might base their volatility forecasts on historical trends or expert opinions, AI models can account for much larger datasets and adapt in real-time to market events. This enables AI-driven portfolios to be better prepared for **market shocks** and **tail risks**.

Example: A study by **BlackRock**, the world's largest asset manager, revealed that machine learning models significantly outperformed traditional **Monte Carlo simulations** for predicting risk-adjusted returns in portfolio management. The AI model, which incorporated a wider range of market data and adjusted predictions on the fly, delivered more accurate forecasts of portfolio risk and potential returns, resulting in **superior portfolio optimization**.

Data Source:

- "Machine Learning and the Future of Portfolio Management," **BlackRock Research**, 2020.

3. Mitigating Behavioral Biases in Investment Decisions

Human investors are often influenced by **cognitive biases**, such as **loss aversion**, **overconfidence**, and **herding behavior**, which can lead to suboptimal investment decisions. AI, however, is **immune** to these biases. By making data-driven, logic-based decisions, AI can avoid the psychological traps that frequently lead to poor investment choices.

Biases in Human Decision-Making

Humans tend to overreact to **short-term market movements** or become overconfident in their predictions. For example, a human investor might panic during a market downturn and sell off assets at a loss, or they might become overly optimistic during a bull market and take on excessive risk. These biases can have a significant negative impact on **risk-adjusted returns**.

AI tools, on the other hand, rely on **objective data** rather than emotions, leading to **more consistent** and **rational decision-making**. For example, an AI system might identify that an asset's price drop is due to a short-term event (e.g., earnings miss) rather than a long-term trend. It would then adjust the portfolio allocation accordingly, without the emotional reactions that could lead a human investor to make irrational decisions.

Example: In 2020, **AlphaGo**, an AI developed by **DeepMind**, beat human world champions at the ancient Chinese game of Go. This milestone highlighted AI's ability to make decisions based on pure logic and data, avoiding biases like **anchoring** (relying too heavily on initial information) or **confirmation bias** (seeking data that supports one's preexisting beliefs). Similarly, in finance, AI-driven portfolios are less prone to these behavioral biases, leading to superior **risk-adjusted returns** over time.

Data Source:

- "The Psychology of Investment: Understanding Biases," **Behavioral Finance Journal**, 2019.

4. Evidence of AI Outperformance in Risk-Adjusted Returns

The effectiveness of AI tools in generating superior risk-adjusted returns is no longer just a theoretical argument—it is backed by data and real-world performance.

- **Hedge Fund Performance**: In 2018, **AQR Capital Management**, a leading hedge fund, published a study comparing AI-driven investment strategies to traditional, human-managed ones. The results showed that AI models outperformed human-managed strategies in terms of both **absolute returns** and **risk-adjusted returns**. Specifically, AI was able to identify long-term trends and avoid costly market downturns, leading to a **higher Sharpe ratio**, a measure of risk-adjusted return.

- **AI-Driven ETFs**: Several exchange-traded funds (ETFs) that rely on AI algorithms have outperformed traditional index funds in recent years. For example, the **AI-Powered Equity ETF (AIEQ)**, launched by **EquBot** and powered by IBM Watson, uses AI to select stocks based on a range of criteria. According to **Morningstar**, AIEQ delivered **outperformance** relative to the S&P 500 in multiple time periods, achieving higher returns with lower volatility, a critical aspect of **risk-adjusted performance**.

Example: **AIEQ** has consistently delivered superior risk-adjusted returns since its launch. As of mid-2021, the fund had outperformed the S&P 500 by a substantial margin, largely due to AI's ability to manage volatility and optimize stock selection in real-time.

Data Source:

- "AI-Powered ETF: A Comparative Analysis," **Morningstar**, 2021.
- "AI vs. Human: Hedge Fund Performance," **AQR Capital Management**, 2018.

5. The Future of AI and Human Collaboration in Risk-Adjusted Performance

While AI tools are outpacing human decision-making in many areas of risk-adjusted returns, it's essential to note that the future of AI in finance is not about replacing humans, but rather about **enhancing human capabilities**. The most successful investment strategies will likely involve **collaborations** between AI-driven insights and human expertise. For example, AI might handle data analysis and risk management, while human professionals focus on strategic decision-making, client relationships, and ethical considerations.

Example: Firms like **Goldman Sachs** and **JP Morgan** have begun using AI tools alongside their human analysts. The combination of human expertise and machine intelligence creates a **hybrid model**

where AI handles the data-heavy tasks, and humans focus on interpreting AI insights within the broader market context.

Conclusion: Embracing AI for Superior Risk-Adjusted Returns

AI has clearly demonstrated its ability to achieve superior **risk-adjusted returns** by processing vast amounts of data, improving predictive accuracy, and mitigating behavioral biases. While traditional human-managed strategies have their place, AI-driven tools are increasingly outperforming them in terms of both **speed** and **precision**. The future of finance will likely involve a symbiotic relationship between human expertise and AI, allowing investors and financial professionals to unlock new levels of performance in their portfolios.

As AI continues to evolve, its potential to revolutionize risk management and investment strategies in finance will only grow, making it an indispensable tool for anyone looking to optimize returns in an increasingly complex market.

Final Conclusion: Thriving in the AI-Powered Future of Finance

As we reach the end of this journey, one key truth becomes abundantly clear: **AI is not a threat to your finance career, but a powerful tool that, when embraced, can propel you to new heights.** The rapidly evolving landscape of finance demands that professionals adapt, learn, and grow in order to stay relevant. Those who choose to leverage AI's capabilities will not only remain employed but will become **indispensable** in their roles—whether as analysts, risk managers, portfolio managers, or financial leaders.

This book has explored how AI will revolutionize the finance industry, not just in terms of automation, but in transforming the **core value** that financial professionals provide. While some aspects of finance, such as data processing, risk assessment, and portfolio optimization, may be increasingly handled by machines, **human judgment, creativity, and strategic thinking** will continue to be essential. AI is here to augment, not replace, your capabilities.

Let's revisit the most powerful takeaways from this book to ensure you can apply them effectively and **future-proof** your career in finance:

1. The Power of Data and AI in Finance

AI's ability to analyze **vast amounts of data** in real-time is revolutionizing financial decision-making. Whether it's **portfolio management**, **fraud detection**, **credit risk assessment**, or **predictive analytics**, AI can process data faster, more accurately, and at a larger scale than any human team.

Key takeaway: **Understand the value of data** and the tools available to you. Even if you don't work directly with AI systems, having **data literacy** will allow you to communicate more effectively with your AI team and leverage these tools to enhance your decision-making.

2. Risk-Adjusted Returns: AI's Superiority in Performance

AI has demonstrated its ability to **optimize risk-adjusted returns** through advanced predictive models, eliminating biases, and processing large datasets. Machine learning algorithms can forecast volatility, identify hidden risks, and optimize portfolios with unparalleled precision.

Key takeaway: **Integrate AI tools into your risk management strategy**. Whether you're a risk manager or portfolio manager, working with AI will enhance your ability to manage **market risks** and achieve higher **risk-adjusted returns** than traditional methods.

3. Lifelong Learning and Adaptability

In a rapidly changing world, one thing is certain: your willingness to **adapt and learn** will define your success. The financial industry is evolving with AI, and those who remain committed to **continuous learning** will stay ahead of the curve. This involves not only learning how AI works but also understanding how it can be applied within your specific role and organization.

Key takeaway: **Never stop learning**. Commit to gaining both **technical knowledge** and **industry insights** to remain indispensable. Take online courses, attend webinars, and stay informed about the latest trends in AI and finance.

4. Developing a Growth Mindset and AI Literacy

Rather than fearing AI, view it as an **opportunity** for growth. By cultivating a **growth mindset**, you embrace change and see it as a tool for improving your efficiency and performance. Additionally, **AI literacy**—understanding the basic concepts of AI, machine learning, and data science—empowers you to collaborate effectively with AI teams and make more informed decisions.

Key takeaway: Develop a **growth mindset** and **AI literacy**. You don't need to become a data scientist, but you do need to understand how AI can enhance your work and help you become more valuable in your role.

5. AI as a Collaborative Partner, Not a Replacement

One of the most powerful themes throughout this book has been that AI should not be feared as a job-stealing force. Instead, **AI is a collaborative partner**. It automates routine tasks, analyzes data at scale, and provides deeper insights, but it still relies on **human judgment** to interpret and apply its findings.

Key takeaway: Work **with AI**, not against it. By leveraging AI tools, you can amplify your skills, increase your efficiency, and enhance your ability to make more strategic, data-driven decisions.

6. Bridging the Gap: Finance and Technology

The future of finance lies at the intersection of **finance expertise** and **technology**. Being able to **speak both languages**—the language of finance and the language of AI—will position you as a leader in your field. Finance professionals who can **collaborate effectively with AI specialists**, understand the tools, and guide their application within the financial context will have the most success in the AI-powered future.

Key takeaway: **Bridge the gap between finance and technology**. Strengthen your communication skills with AI teams, and contribute your financial expertise to help design AI tools that solve real business problems.

7. AI's Role in Ethical Decision-Making and Regulatory Compliance

As AI becomes integral to finance, the importance of **ethical AI** and **compliance** grows. AI can be prone to biases, and it's up to finance professionals to ensure that AI systems operate ethically, transparently, and in compliance with regulations.

Key takeaway: **Prioritize ethics and compliance** when working with AI. Be an advocate for fair, transparent, and explainable AI systems, ensuring that the tools you use meet **regulatory standards** and don't inadvertently harm stakeholders.

8. Building a Resilient Career in an AI-Driven World

AI is inevitable, but so is the need for **human leadership, strategy, and decision-making**. The future belongs to finance professionals who can **adapt**, **innovate**, and **lead** in this AI-powered environment. Those who continuously upskill, embrace AI, and focus on developing their **emotional intelligence** and **strategic insight** will thrive in the new world of finance.

Key takeaway: **Become a resilient leader**. Embrace change, focus on lifelong learning, and position yourself as someone who **combines human expertise with AI-driven insights** to create value for your organization.

Final Thought: AI Isn't the Future; It's the Present

AI is already changing the landscape of finance, and its impact will only grow in the coming years. It's not something you can afford to ignore or hope will go away. The time to embrace it is now. The finance professionals who understand and leverage AI will become **more efficient, more effective**, and **more indispensable**.

To remain **relevant** and **competitive**, take actionable steps today: **learn AI basics, embrace AI tools, upskill continuously**, and **collaborate effectively** with AI and data science teams. The future of finance is not one of AI versus humans, but of AI and humans working **together** to shape a smarter, more dynamic financial world.

As you look toward the future, remember that **AI is your ally**, not your adversary. By leveraging it wisely and working with it to enhance your skills, you can unlock new opportunities and thrive in an AI-driven finance world.

The road ahead is bright for those who are prepared, adaptable, and ready to embrace the future with AI as their partner.

About the Author:

Hudson Budrick III spent nearly three decades on Wall Street as a complex derivatives and structured products trader, private equity investor and entrepreneur. Budrick has launched several data driven start-ups. He resides in Manhattan with his family and beloved cats.

www.ingramcontent.com/pod-product-compliance
Lightning Source LLC
Chambersburg PA
CBHW070351230526
45471CB00006B/2523